My Life with God

Ronald Nelson

ISBN: 979-8-89075-604-6

Contents

Preamble

The purpose of this autobiography is to record the frequent times of God's moments in my life. In looking back at these moments, I recall what He called me to do and what I did, as well as other memories of my life. In retrospect, the God's presence seems to be always there through all my life. I realize that God has never missed a moment being at my side.

Perhaps it was also my Guardian Angel, the Blessed Virgin Mary, or the Trinity of God, my family, or my relatives who have prayed for me and made me who I am today and over the years.

I was urged many times by a good friend, Father Gregory Johnson, to record this information because he said, *I had so many good and interesting stories* to share. I hope you find the stories in the following pages as interesting as he did and possibly healing for you and your loved ones.

Chapter 1

In the Beginning!

The story of my life begins on October 17, 1938. I was born in Faribault, Minnesota, which was named after Alexander Faribault, a French-Canadian fur trapper. Faribault, as I would later come to find out, established an Indian Trading Post at the confluence of the Straight River and the Cannon River, which then flows toward the North, and eventually to the Mississippi River.

I was baptized two weeks after my birth by Father John Patrick Foley at Immaculate Conception Catholic Church. From what I have been told of the ceremony by my mother, the baptism was held outdoors on a warm October afternoon in a garden area of the church. The garden was focused on point under the shadow of a man-made grotto dedicated to and containing a statue of the Blessed Virgin Mary in Her Immaculate Conception pose. Her image looked directly on the event of my baptism. Now, years after my that beautiful event, she still hasn't stopped looking out for my family and me.

The baptism was attended by my parents, Marie Elizabeth Nelson and Edwin Julius Nelson, Super Value owner, William Thompson Lund, blacksmith and Anna (Dusek) Lund my lovely maternal grandparents from Blooming Prairie Minnesota and Aunt Edith and Eddie Wanous also from Blooming Prairie.

I was later confirmed and received the Eucharist in the same church during grade school. I attended Catholic Schools next to the Church (Immaculate Conception Grade School), and Catholic High School (Bethlehem Academy, BA) across the street from the Grade School, and the College of St. Thomas in St. Paul, Minnesota.

I also attended the University of Minnesota Dental School earning my dental degree (DDS) and, later, the University of Iowa Dental Graduate School in Iowa City, Iowa earning a Masters Degree (MS) in Dental Education.

Growing up as an only child, I spent countless hours alone in my home while my parents were away at work. Surprisingly, I found myself drawn to the solitude and never once felt bored or complained. During the school week, I kept myself occupied with homework, ensuring that my time alone was productive and fulfilling. I worked summers in my Dad's grocery store as well as the Faribault Canning Company and the Faribault Woolen Mills. I also caddied at the Faribault Golf and Country Club on Sundays.

Despite our small family, we were extremely close-knit and rarely experienced any conflict or arguments. I have fond memories of my maternal grandparents visiting us every weekend from their small hometown of Blooming Prairie, Minnesota. My grandfather was a skilled blacksmith and a first-generation immigrant from Denmark, while my grandmother was a first-generation immigrant Czech who worked at the Cozy Inn, a local café. My paternal grandparents Ragna and

Obert Nelson lived just a mile away and we saw them often. After grandpa Obert died Ragna married Andy Anderson a salesman. They were all first-generation Norwegian immigrants.

Sports were a big part of my life, and I easily made friends throughout grade school, high school, and even in college. In high school I played football in the fall, basketball in the winter, and golf in the spring, all while attending Immaculate Conception grade school and BA high school. Both schools were located next to our church, Immaculate Conception Parish, and were staffed by the Dominican Sisters of Sinsinawa, Wisconsin.

When I was in fourth and fifth grade, my family moved to Decorah, Iowa, where my father was transferred to work with the Piggly Wiggly grocery chain. Our house was situated next to a vast forest that stretched for miles around the town. This is where I fell in love with nature and all its wonders. I would spend hours outside, exploring the woods and marveling at the beauty of a quiet forest, the small plants, and the small animals. During the summer, a seasonal river ran through town from snow melt, but when it dried up, I would hunt for agates and Indian arrow heads that had washed down from the hills during the Spring season. My agate and arrow- head collection grew to be rather large. I had a hard time with word spelling, and I remember taking words home to write down twenty times in my notebook while my Mother helped me.

On the weekends, my parents often entertained their friends in our home, I would stay up late in my bedroom listening to them sing in perfect harmony.

During my Dad's career in the grocery business he was asked to manage a Piggly Wiggly store in Decorah, Iowa, and was eventually asked to manage three stores simultaneously in Iowa. After two years and that ridiculous promotion(?) he quit the Piggly Wiggly career position, moved back to Faribault where he purchased the neighborhood grocery store/home next to Garfield Grade School, where he had attended for his grade school learning.

Our home was located in the back of the store, just two blocks from my schools and church. During the summers, I participated in Garfield Grade School's arts, crafts, and sports programs, where I made my mother a bracelet out of plastic yarn and won the City Badminton Championship and the City Yoyo Championship in one unforgettable summer.

Chapter 2

Youth

It is often said that childhood is the happiest time of a person's life. While I like to think of my life as an amalgamation of wonderful moments bathed in God's light, this is certainly true as far as my childhood was concerned. Not only did I enjoy myself as a child, I have many wonderful memories from this time, which I can recall with vivid details even now!

I remember having a lot of interesting adventures between the ages of nine to thirteen. I loved to hunt and spent many Saturdays, during the summers *and* winters, hunting along the Straight River on the outskirts of Faribault.

I had a 22-caliber rifle to hunt with, and how I acquired the rifle was a story in itself. I hadn't purchased the rifle, in fact, I had won it by selling newspaper "starts" for the Saint Paul Pioneer Press and Dispatch.

In the summer, I hunted for squirrels, while in the winter, I hunted rabbits. However, as much as I loved hunting, I simply enjoyed being outdoors and breathing in fresh, clean air. It didn't matter what activity I was doing, as long as I was breathing in-and- out the smog free air of the pristine the Minnesota countryside. I was happy.

Some other activities that I enjoyed included ice skating in the winter. The city would pump water onto the tennis courts at Wapacuta Park, just a block from where my parents and I lived on Third Avenue South in the small local neighborhood grocery store attached to the front of our home.

At Wapacuta Park, the kids flocked to the ice-skating rink in the winter despite the below-zero Minnesota weather. When you got too cold skating in that freezing weather, you could go into the "warming house—" a temporary house trailer set up just to gather and warm up by the wood-burning stove and tighten the laces on your skates and talk with friends. I remember kissing a girl for the first time outside by that trailer.

After I kissed her, I realized she had snot running down from her nose to her lips, so my first kiss was technically a wet kiss! *Ugh.*

At age twelve or thirteen, I won the Yoyo twirling contest for the City of Faribault. Later that summer, I won the City of Faribault badminton tournament. I guess you could say that I liked— or perhaps excelled is the better word here— in sports.

Another memory that I recall fondly from my early teenage years are the Dominican Sisters of Sinsinawa, Wisconsin, who ran our grade and high schools, taught and ruled over us. Although they weren't what you could call "strict," they could occasionally be harsh. At that time, they wore the full habit, which I and others described them as the "covered wagon."

Apart from the Dominican Sisters, and sports, my other interest included music. I took piano lessons from an older sister (Stella) who would keep time with my piano playing by clicking her dentures together to keep the rhythm. I also took coronet lessons and was in the Grade School and High School band.

Later, as a freshman at my High School (BA), I joined the band doing all the percussion instruments (snare drums, cymbals, bells, etc.). Moreover, I'd also joined the orchestra and played the tympani drums and other percussion toys. There was much to enjoy in the orchestra, but what I loved the most was playing John Phillip Susa's military marches.

As much as I loved music and playing, I retired from all band and orchestra involvement my sophomore year when I realized it would interfere with sports. I guess at that age, I finally had to pick between my two loves, and I chose sports.

Chapter 3

Reality

Sister Carroll was my seventh-grade teacher at I.C. Her face was chubby, and she had dark eyebrows that, when curled up, could give you that fierce "nun look." If you are my BA classmate reading this, you'd find yourself smiling at the mention of the nun look, since you would know exactly what I meant. For everyone else, however, you're free to come up with another explanation. In any case, the "nun look" meant trouble.

Sister Carroll had the unique ability to smell trouble from miles away. One time, she caught me burning my initials on my desktop with a small magnifying glass. In my defense, the sun was coming into our classroom at just the perfect angle— I had to make use of all that sunlight!

She saw the smoke, slammed the ruler she held on the top of my hands (which hurt!), grabbed me by my ear, and marched me to the principal's office. As I recall, I was sent home to explain to my mother why I was home early. But it turned out, fate had other plans for me. I went home early to find it empty. As it turned out, my mother was at work in my father's grocery store. By that point, the grocery story was a large Super Value store on 2nd Avenue and 5th Street in Faribault.

After school that same day, I snuck into the gym, changed clothes, and participated in basketball practice, which was coached by Fr. Frank McGrade, a good friend of my parents. He was also very social and played golf with my father, as did Father Dillon. At that time, we had three priests at I.C. church to serve our Catholic community. Our priest coach, however, went to dances with my parents and danced with as many ladies as possible. I know because I was usually there. At that time in the '50s, the parish had three priests assigned, including the Pastor, Father John Patrick Foley, Father McGrade associate priest and Fr. Dillon associate priest. After WWII, there were many priestly vocations in the church. Father McGrade was a party man but also a good priest. He came into our grade and high school to all grades and taught classes in religion.

But coming back to Sister Caroll, one day I came home, and there she was, sitting in our living room, chatting away with my mother. She had a cocktail in one hand, and a lit cigarette in the other which she was smoking.

*Why's a nun doing tha*t? I thought.

I avoided any conversation and ducked into my bedroom as quickly as I could and started to do my homework.

My mother told me after Sister Carroll left that she said,

"I was an excellent student and was an angel in class." Even after my desk burning episode!

I stared at my mother with my eyes wide open with shock. You just never know what the next surprise is going to be! God laughs, too!

Sports

Anyway, as I mentioned earlier, I excelled in sports in grade school and high school and intra-murals during pre-dental and dental school. When I attended BA high school, I played all of the sports available in our small school. I have fond memories of Tom Paul our basketball and football coach; Dewey Van Orsow the B-Squad basketball coach and Assistant Scout leader along with Tom Healy Scout Master. My mom and Dad both played golf in the summer and bowling in the Winter. I guess you could say that we were a sports-loving family.

In Dental School, I was on the bowling team and played intermural basketball, cross-country running, and slow-pitch softball, and that was all I had time for. In predental studies at St. Thomas College (now the University of St. Thomas), just across the Bridge over the Mississippi River to St. Paul from the Dental School, I was tempted to play college football and basketball, but I was commuting 100 miles round trip each daily from Faribault. After much consideration, I had no choice but to come to the dreadful conclusion; sports just wasn't practical for me anymore!

Girls

All throughout high school, I took different girls to school dances, like the Snowball, Homecoming, and Prom. I didn't have much desire to go out with one girl except Carroll Shaft, whose mother rejected me because I was a Catholic (Can you believe that?) So, at the end of that summer, we had to stop seeing each other. She took ballet lessons, and I got to attend one of her Minneapolis recitals. She was the Prima Donna Ballerina for that concert and was really a good ballet dancer.

During the other summers, I dated a few girls but spent most of my time hanging out with John Studer. We were best friends and did a lot of naughty things together but never got caught. We started smoking cigarettes together in ninth grade. We remained friends all through grade school and high school. After graduating from Notre Dame, he attended and graduated from a local night law school just across the street from St. Thomas in St. Paul. As I had decided earlier, as soon as school started in the fall, I quit dating because school was more important to me.

Chapter 4

Luci

College was an exciting time for me. Not only was I transitioning into adulthood, but this was the time in my life where I would meet the woman who would come to be the love of my life.

Her name was Lucille (Luci) Jewett, and I met her in the winter of 1956 during my first year in college. She was a Junior at (B.A.), my alma mater. One weekend when I was home from college, I played in an alumni basketball game and scored the winning basket as time expired. As fun as that was, that was the weekend that I noticed Luci playing in the band during the game.

Pretty girl. I thought to myself and smiled.

While this was the first time that I saw her, nothing happened then. However, on another weekend when I was home watching a B.A. basketball game, I was approached by my friend Tom Van Orsow, at half time.

Tom and I had played football and basketball together at B.A., and I liked him. We were good friends although he was a year behind me in school. He suggested that since he had a date and no car and I had a car and no date, I should get a date and we could cruise around town after the game and stop off at the Ice Cream Store. The Ice Cream Store was a local B.A. high school hang out. I always ordered a cherry coke and fries. Toward the end of the game, I went down the stairs to the basketball floor and looked up and saw Luci again. She stood there playing her clarinet in the B.A. school band, wearing their Cardinal Red uniform, and I remembered her. She was the cute girl from the earlier game.

At the end of the game, I went up the stairs to where she was seated and said,

"Can I take you home after the game?"

"I just live across the street, ha-ha!" She smiled and answered.

So, I told her that we were going to cruise around downtown Faribault in my car with Tom Van Orso and his girlfriend. After that would go to the ice cream store for cherry cokes and maybe fries.

"Alright, but I have to go home and change out of my band uniform first." she said with excitement in her eyes.

I nodded my head in a yes, and we got up and left.

The Ice Cream Store was packed with BA game attendees, but we found a booth. We had a great time. I noticed that one of Luci's classmates (RB) kept looking at me the whole time we were there. Later at other school events, I caught her staring at me often and I started to wonder why. After one BA event I asked her if I could give her a ride home and she agreed. At the door I decided to kiss her. She opened her mouth and kissed me with a very wet kiss. I did not like that and decided she was not a girl for me. That was my second "wet" kiss and I didn't like either of them. No more of her and that stuff!

***

As you can probably guess, Luci and I saw each other a lot during that school year on weekends and eventually fell in love. The following summer, Luci and I eloped and were headed toward California to join our friends Mike Mullen, a year ahead of me at BA and JoAnn Lockmann, a Faribault High School graduate. Much like us, they had also eloped. We got as far as Mesa, Arizona and were stopped by a police car for speeding in a school zone.

After a few minutes, the police figured out that we were on the run. I tried to explain to them, but they weren't having any of it. They put me in a lock up and I soon saw that I was the only gringo there. Scary!!

Just from the way that they were looking at me, I could tell that they had nothing but the worst intentions in their mind. Although I was terrified, to this day, I thank God that nothing happened. *Whew!*

I was released the next day and told that Luci was already on a Greyhound bus headed to Minnesota, which meant that I had to drive home alone. When I got home, my mother was in the shower and ran out when she heard my voice. As her emotions got the best of her, she hugged me wet and naked. My father never said a word. I guess because he and my mother had also eloped to Iowa when they were young. Luci's mother immediately sent Luci up to the Centical Retreat House in Minneapolis as soon as she got home for a weekend retreat. When she got home, Luci said "everything would be alright." She didn't want to add any further details, but I was curious. I wanted to know what this priest had told her, so I went up to the retreat house and knocked on the door.

The priest, Jesuit Father John J Campbell opened the door and after I told him who I was and who Luci was, he invited me in. I stayed there for three days, called my parents, told them where I was, and asked them not to worry.

Throughout these three days, Father Campbell and I talked and talked and I learned a lot about life, God and difficulties along the way and how to deal with them. Father "Jack" became one of our best friends and Luci and I had him as a house guest many times when he could take some respite time off no matter where we were in the Navy by then. The last time I saw him he was in a Jesuit retirement house in St. Louis, Missouri and he was still the jovial, *shock-you-by-what-he-said* type of guy. Even after all these years, his sense of humor hadn't left him.

Some days, after I'd told him all about myself and what I had been up to, he'd sit me down and tell me how he was feeling.

"Some mornings, I feel so bad that I think I'm an Atheist,"

He took a small pause, and then continued and smiled,

"However, by noon, I'm and Agnostic,

Another pause,

and by dinner I feel better and I'm a Christian again."

I couldn't help but smile. Even now, as I'm writing about him, I can't help but giggle a little. I guess Father Jack was just one-of-a-kind. For as long as I'm here, I'm certain that I'll never forget that man. We both loved him. He is probably cracking jokes in Heaven to this day.

Life Partner

As for Luci and I, the rest became history. Luci and I were married during Thanksgiving break during college on November 28, 1957. I felt very fortunate to have found Luci and she became my soulmate and the love of my life. As time passed on, my love for her only grew as we had children together. I knew that we would spend our lives together despite the highs and lows of our relationship (very normal) and all the challenges and difficulties of life that we faced together. Throughout the ups, the downs, the light and darkness, I'll always love my Luci.

Chapter 5

Maturing

Before I met my Luci, however, I was just a typical teenager who didn't pay attention to much—except for girls and sports, all throughout high school. I graduated when I was seventeen years old. Oftentimes, in high school, the Dominican Sisters would take us to the church, Immaculate Conception, during the school day to pray the rosary, or for Holy Mass or for Adoration or all of the above. Back then, I didn't pay much attention to any of these exposures to God and His Church, but now as I look back and reflect on that time in my life, I realize how much influence that those experiences had in shaping me to the person that I am right now. I now can thank those Dominican sisters who made a huge impact in my life and the lives of my classmates although we were young and immature it was not something I took seriously at the time at the time.

During my sophomore year at BA, we a took a scholastic aptitude exam and I scored high in Medicine, Dentistry, Law and Journalism. Coincidently those were the four professions that I had thought about a lot recently and here they showed up as high ranking on my SAT test. That's when I decided to be a dentist. My father wanted me to go into the grocery business with him, like my two cousins, Jim and Jerry Nelson, (Their father being my Uncle Clarence) but I had only worked in the Super Value store for a few summers at a measly $.50 cents an hour and did not have enough experience or desire for that business. I also worked two summers in the local Canning Factory at $1.00 per hour, processing butter kernel corn and peas. Another summer, I worked for Jolly Green Giant out in the country in the field harvesting peas 16 hours per day (which was how long my shift typically lasted) by pitching pea vines into a big machine that separated the peas from the silage.

At the Jolly Green Giant fields site, large dump trucks brought loads of just harvested pea vines to the canning factory twenty-four hours a day. To this day, it remains the hardest job that I've ever had. A group of us got the job because Tom Paul, our football coach, worked with the Green Giant company in summers, and thought that it would "toughen us up" for football in the fall. My hard work wasn't for nothing however because after that summer of slavery, I was finally able to buy my first car— a 1949 Ford for $400.00 in 1955.

As I mentioned earlier, I worked one summer in the Faribault Woolen Mills. My work friend, a high school classmate, was Dick Paquette, and we were partners. Our job was to tear blankets into 82" length pieces from 100 hundred yard-long rolls all summer. We got so far ahead of the sewing machine ladies, who attached labels and folded the blankets that we had to stop working. Our reward was two days off with no pay, which in all honesty, wasn't that much of a reward in my mind. Dick, who was also going to St. Thomas, came to me one day at school and said he was considering becoming a priest.

We had a long talk, and I did not try to talk him into becoming or not becoming a priest, but we did a lot of soul searching. He eventually earned his teaching degree and got married and went to Belgium to teach in the American School in Antwerp. Another classmate friend at B.A. was Pete Johnson, whose father was the CEO and president of the Faribault Woolen Mills. Pete eventually took over after working in the sales field for many years. Pete and I also played on the B.A. golf team together during four years at B.A. My best friend John Studer also played football, basketball and golf right along with me.

Chapter 6

Education

I did well academically in grade school, high school, college and in dental school. As far as I was concerned, the process of applying to colleges was a straightforward one. After high school, I had only applied to two colleges—Notre Dame in Indiana and St. Thomas college in St Paul, Minnesota. After waiting for a couple of weeks, I got accepted into St. Thomas. It didn't take much thought for me, since I received my rejection letter from Notre Dame a couple of days later. My rejection letter stated, in clear and concise wording, that my GPA was too low, with an 86 average. Strangely enough, 87 would be a B average, and would have been considered good enough to be accepted. God had a plan for me. I guess the difference between acceptance and rejection resided in that one-point difference but as Luci would say "God is in Charge."

At college, I spent my first-year rooming off campus with Mike Mullen. Looking at it now, I can tell how bad of a choice that was. Mike was a terrible influence on me, and together, the both of us got into a lot of bad situations. For example, the first week of college, Mike and I were in a bar in downtown Minneapolis, when suddenly the police barged in the front and back doors, yelling,

"It's a raid! Stay where you are!"

Mike and I got out the front door after the initial group of officers came in and overran our booth which was next to the front door. We ran out and down the street. My car, however, was parked in front of the bar. We waited about an hour and approached the car thinking the coast was clear but were immediately arrested. We were taken to the city jail, fingerprinted and told to call our parents. I spent the night in jail and had to pay to get my car out of the impound lot. As you can probably imagine, my parents were not happy at all, and from the next day onwards, I had to leave my car in Faribault, and hitch a ride daily to college in St Paul with an editor of a national magazine whose office and printing facility was located there.

My best friend of high school, John Studer, had been accepted into Notre Dame, and as we started college, we had to split up. John ended up being a Navy lawyer and eventually became a judge. We often took cigarettes from his mom's pack and smoked all through high school. I quit smoking after I got in the Navy and when the Surgeon General told the world how injurious smoking was for your health. After hearing the words come out of his mouth, I could never continue smoking as I did before. John, on the other hand, never did quit. He passed away with complications from lung cancer in 2018 at the age of 79.

To come back to St. Thomas, however, although my first week at college had been nothing short of a tumultuous rollercoaster ride, I still managed to earn high grades in pre-dentistry. During my first class in inorganic chemistry, I was very encouraged because I got the highest grade of 35 students. I also got an A in Organic Chemistry along with a string of A's and B's in all the other courses that I was taking. As far as I remember, the only C I got was in physics.

While at St. Thomas a young priest was selected to be the President of the school. He was the youngest president ever at that time. He had also been a undergraduate student at St. Thomas before he entered the St. Paul Seminary, where I was later trained to be a Deacon. He was also elected "Mr. Tommy" unanimously by the student body for his popularity as student body president, sports success, a clean life and had a 4.0 grade point average. Needless to say, he was an extremely charismatic guy, which accounted for his popularity.

As president of St. Thomas, he was also very liked and admired as well. He called many assemblies of the student body together to encourage them in their studies, their search for God, and to urge them to be true to their selves and their school activities. I attended mass often on campus at noon when I didn't have class, because of his influence. While I was at St. Thomas he was selected as the youngest Auxiliary Bishop in the St. Paul Diocese and had to leave the campus for Bishop duties. Once he took his leave, everyone felt his absence void in the space all around us, but eventually, we all moved on with our lives.

A few years later, however, I heard news of the former President. He had found himself in the middle of a serious problem and dilemma with a Papal Encyclical concerning how the church should respond to women who had an abortion and or birth control. His main point, borrowing from Jesus's teachings, was to forgive especially in the confessional or during personal counseling. The backlash that he received was so intense that eventually, he had to resign his position as Bishop. He even moved away from Minnesota. Instead of Bishop duties, he became a Professor of Religion at the University of New Mexico. I was so sad that I cried for days. He not only was a good man, a good priest, but also a very brave man who stood up for what he believed in. He was my hero.

In 1959, I was accepted to the Dental School at the University of Minnesota and graduated with a BS in 1961, and DDS in 1963. I spent my first and second year at continuing my Bachelor of Science studies, as well as the Dental studies. I worked in a girl's Sorority during the first year with one other male student setting up the tables for dinner, serving and clearing off the tables, and washing the dishes after the meal was finished and girls left. Our pay was the evening meal which was the same as what the girls ate. I remember there always being a lot to eat since the cook made sure that she always made enough for us.

Although I appreciated how caring some people at college could be, one thing I definitely could do without was how large the University of Minnesota truly was. For the most part, it was an overwhelming feeling that took a hold on me each time that I attended class with 500 students in attendance. Moreover, I couldn't concentrate on what the professor was saying at all, because the chatter of everyone else attending was too distracting.

During my first year, in dental school, I stayed in a dental fraternity house, Psi Omega. I went home to Faribault on weekends. During my sophomore year, Luci and I, along with our three kids moved into married student housing, which consisted of WWII Quonset hut near the university campus. The huts were long enough so that two families could live back-to-back with a partition to separate them. However, as you can probably imagine, there wasn't much privacy to be had. The walls were thin and we could always hear the neighbor's beds squeaking when they were active. With three children to take care of, we were maxed at out our end, but we were happy. Eventually Luci was pregnant with our 4th child, Ron Jr. who was delivered during our first year in the Navy Dental Corps at the Naval Training Center at Great Lakes, Illinois.

During the winter, I had to cover the windows in the Quonset hut with plastic sheets because the wind blew through the poorly fitting windows right on our heads in bed. We attended a lot of University of Minnesota Gofer football games, and the stadiums was always full with fifty thousand fans yelling their heads off. Minnesota won the Big 10 conference two years in a row and qualified to go to the Rose Bowl those two years. On game day, we would park at the Psi Omega fraternity house which was my Dental School fraternity and walk to the stadium and often had a few oranges injected with vodka for our entertainment during the game. I remember the babysitter cost $.50 cents an hour, which back then, was a lot of money. Now the cost of babysitters, I hear, is minimum wage rate or more.

Anyway, with all that being said, I made lifetime friends during my years associated with the fraternity and the dental school and I treasure these friendships in my heart, although most of them have passed away now. Kermit Olsen, was a big influence in my life. He was an older veteran and a helicopter pilot from the Korean War era. We studied together for most of our exams. He also taught me how to share my time and possessions with others, which as an only child, was a difficult lesson for me to learn. Every time we gathered to study in his apartment, we smoked cigars and totally filled the place with cigar smoke. His wife Ann had to wash all the clothes the next day and was she mad. We quit smoking cigars after that. We both did really well on those exams that we studied for together and it was worth the effort. One time however, we had 6 exams in 2 days, and it was impossible to study for all of them in a limited time limit. To be prepared sufficiently I studied many days in advance in order to pass the exams.

Chapter 7

Military Service

Upon graduation, I immediately entered the Navy Dental Corps as a Lieutenant on June 15, 1963, and my first duty station was at Great Lakes, Illinois. President Kennedy was assassinated that November 22, 1963, during our tour at Great Lakes. The base was huge and served as a naval recruit training center, with thousands of recruits there in basic training, and hundreds in specialty training "A" schools.

During this time, the Vietnam War was just getting started.

The training center was located along side Lake Superior, and I was invited a few times to go out in Captain Harris Keene's boat to fish and swim. He was the Director of the Navy Research Center at Great Lakes, which just so happened to be in the same building where I worked.

Captain Harris had four associate research specialists who were also dentists plus staff. There were approximately eighty clinical dentists at the Training Center, including me, to take care of all the oral needs of the recruits and students. Because I was friendly with Captain Harris Keene, I was recruited to work in research for about six months. I worked with two other dentists on a project called "Greater Utilization of Dental Technicians." The goal of the study was to see if a Dental technician could place quality amalgam fillings in the teeth of recruits after the dentist had anesthetized the patient and made the tooth preparation removing the decay. Three groups were studied for quality of the restoration: 1. The dental technician's quality of restoration who knew they were judged for quality. 2. The dentist quality of their restoration who knew they were being judged. 3. The quality of the dentist's restoration who did not know they were being judged.

The technicians were the best restorers in that study. *Go figure!*

The loser of the three groups being tested were the dentists who did not know that their fillings were being judged. *Makes you wonder!*

During this time, our neighbors were Audrey and Richard Ward, who was a Senior Chief Fireman. He was a coin collector and got me into the habit of collecting coins as well. Another neighbor, a chief also, showed me how to make home brew beer and dandelion wine. The beer had a good taste, and the wine was just so-so. During our 2nd time stationed at Great Lakes in 1973, ten years after our first assignment, we connected with Audrey Ward again and found out Richard had passed away. During that time, we made our only trip to Medjugoria, Yugoslavia where the Blessed Mother Mary was appearing to 6 local children almost daily. We took Audrey with us. Audrey was very touched by the whole experience and although a Methodist, she started saying the daily rosary after we bought her a blessed rosary in Medjugoria. After that visit we spent a few days in Paris, France and in London, England.

Luci had our 4ᵗʰ child, Ron Jr., delivered on September 4, 1963 at the Great Lakes Naval Hospital. Our other children were Debra Ann born on June 24, 1958: Michael William born on June 16, 1959 and Sharon Marie born July 14, 1960. All three were born at District 1 Hospital in Faribault, Minnesota. I think my dad paid the Dr. and hospital costs. Cost for a delivery at the Great Lakes Naval Hospital was $7.00 in advance per birth which I paid!

Just like everything else that she did, Luci delivered the babies very quickly, often 20-30 minutes after arriving at the hospital. The record stood…no attending OBGYN MD or family Doctor made it in time for Luci's deliveries. Luci loved speed in everything she did and couldn't sit still. She always had a deep love for education and when the children were old enough, she started volunteering at the Great Lakes Naval Hospital in the OBGYN clinic seeing new mothers and expectant mothers. She told me that she didn't like the sight of blood but soon she applied for training as an LPN nurse at Lake County Community College nearby in Fox Lake, Illinois. She met a good friend and study mate Annetta Cox, who was recently recovering from the loss of her fiancé in a fatal airplane crash. They became dear friends and studied weekly together. During the second year Annetta was in a serious car accident and broke both of her wrists and we brought her home to live with us until she got her casts off and could function somewhat normally. Luci bathed, fed her and dressed her for a month. Presently, after all these years, Luci and Annetta, who still remains unmarried, remain in touch. They exchange Christmas cards with one-another, and catch up on news and gossip. I do the Christmas cards and letters now that Luci is not able to and keep contact with her.

During our first tour at Great Lakes, it was discernment time for Luci and me to decide if we were going to stay in the Navy or get out and go into private practice back home in Faribault which my father thought we should do. We decided to stay in the Navy, and I augmented into the "Regular Navy" in the Spring of 1964. We went on to many interesting and exciting duty stations which I will describe in the succeeding chapters.

My reasoning for staying in the Navy was I thought I would get bored and stale living in the same town where I was born and raised. Luci felt the same way. In addition, we were both the adventurous types and believed the Navy would help us to see the world and have many experiences that we would not have if we stayed in Faribault. Another consideration, which was personal to me is that I was always considered and referred to as "Eddie Nelson's Son' Which made me feel like a non-entity. I wanted to make a name for myself and be an independent person not someone's son.

I was not surprised by this "Son" designation because my father was very well known in Faribault as he was born and raised there and was a champion in golf, as well as a successful businessman in the grocery business. He also had a very warm and caring personality. So off we went!!

Chapter 8

Sea Duty

Almost immediately, after I augmented into the regular Navy, I received orders to a ship, the USS Bryce Canyon, AD-36, a destroyer tender, home ported in Long Beach and which was deployed to Pearl Harbor, Hawaii for 6-month assignments. We moved to California to the suburb Los Alamitos. After settling in our new home, the ship left for Hawaii. That deployment was our first family separation, but Luci's sister Margaret came to live with her while I was gone. She also baby sat the children when Luci came to Hawaii for two weeks for a visit. To stay busy and to fulfill one of her dreams, Luci applied and was accepted to the John Robert Powers School of modeling in Los Angeles. She did well and upon graduation from the modeling school she was hired and did a lot of live modeling in the Hollywood area. She also took a course in Interior Decoration but did not follow up on that career. Her sister Margaret got a job as a dental assistant and eventually married Dr. Bill Edel.

The Bryce Canyon had three dentists, three technicians and one LPO 1st class dental tech on board. During our deployment Luci was very active in the Fleet Officers Wife's Club in Long Beach as their director of activities. She organized and directed more than one fashion show during my two years on the Ship. She also arranged to have Ronald Regan, who was considering running for Governor of California as a guest speaker at one event. Our first senior dentist was a periodontist, Commander Robert Elliot. I started playing golf every Wednesday in the Fleet Golf League when we were in port and enjoyed playing many different courses in Southern California. Since I was missing one-day of work each week, I was warned that if the golfing on Wednesdays continued, I would have to start working on Saturdays. This would disrupt everything, including my dental assistant's day off. I immediately saw the handwriting on the wall and decided that my Navy career was more important than playing golf, so I quit playing and bit my tongue. The second senior dentist was a trained prosthodontist who was studying and preparing for his boards. It was hard work on the Ship and always very noisy, but we all enjoyed Hawaii, especially when our wives came to visit.

Captain Harris Keene and his wife Susan, who was now the Commanding Officer of the Dental Clinic and the Marine Corp Base in Kaneohe, Hawaii and was previously the Head of the Research Facility at Great Lakes, invited Luci and me to spend a full Saturday with them when Luci was visiting me in Hawaii. In the afternoon, Harris and I went scuba diving and saw a huge Manta Ray which was curious about us and circled around us three times and then smoothly glided away like a big bird. Our Ship was tied up to the pier at Ford Island, near the USS Missouri and I learned to play tennis after work and enjoyed the sport and the exercise.

There was a small Officers club next to the tennis court and spent a couple evenings at the bar with shipmates exchanging sea stories and other adventures we had experienced in Life.

I made good friendships while on board but never crossed paths with them again since they were "line officers" and were destined to do much more sea duty then I was. I became good friends with the medical officer, however, Dennis Busby, but after we departed the ship, we never met again. I understand that he is presently engaged in his medical practice in Santa Barbara, California.

In order to get off Ford Island to go into Waikiki, or to go snorkeling in Hanama Bay, which I did often, we had to take a ferry from Ford Island. The last ferry back to Ford Island and my ship left at 1am. I missed it one time and had to sleep in my car, a vintage red Triumph TR3 with wire wheels and a "rag top." My pride and joy. I didn't sleep well in that small sports car.

I promised Luci that we would go back to Hawaii again someday to live and we did.

My second senior Dental Officer on the Bryce Canyon wrote a letter to me after he left the Navy and suggested that I get out of the Navy and invited me to join him in his practice in California. I wasn't sure if he was the kind of person that I would like to be associated with, so I declined. I was looking forward to many more adventures in the Navy, not stuck in a monotonous private practice in California or Minnesota.

Chapter 9

After Four Children

Luci continued modeling and running modeling shows but still had a yen for more education. While I was at the National Naval Medical Center as the Assistant Dean, she attended American University in Washington DC and eventually earned her B.S. in Nursing. After retirement from the Navy, when we moved back to Hawaii, she started school immediately again and earned her first master's degree in public health nursing and followed that up with another master's degree in Maternal Child Health, Nurse Practitioner. She is a "can do" woman.

Her education got her interesting and productive positions in the medical industry in Hawaii. Eventually, ownership of an ambulatory Care Home in Faribault, Minnesota, called the "Inn Town House, where she and her nurse friend Malia Kelso took care of 12 residents. I think it was the highlight of her nursing career. We eventually sold our half of the home to Malia for $100,000.00. More about our return to Faribault later.

Concerning my military career, I went up the ranks on schedule and eventually retired as a Navy Captain With 26 and 4+ months of active duty in 1985 from Idaho Falls, Idaho. Now as writing this autobiography it has been 40 years since I retired from the Navy. My last duty station and one of the best. More details to follow concerning our different duty stations and adventures around the world.

Chapter 10

Navy Life

In July 1966, we were transferred to NAAS (Naval Auxiliary Air Station) Fallon, Nevada, where another dentist, Captain Jay Shaw, and I took care of the medical and dental staff members, aviators, families and support staff of the base It was a combined Navy and Air Force base whose primary duties to support aviation target practice in the surrounding desert and to provide dental support to the flight squadrons who would fly in from the West Coast aircraft carriers, Naval Air Stations, and Air Force bases on the West Coast and other places to participate in various bombing opportunities and practice in the Arco desert surrounding Fallon.

Dr. Shaw was studying and doing research to become a Board-Certified Endodontist. One day after work at happy hour, he shared with me that he was born and raised a Mormon. I asked him if he still went to the Mormon Stake House or Temple services, and he said, "No, because that church and its beliefs are a lie." I was shocked! He did not believe Mormonism was a religion, but a cult, that believed in so called revelations from God and the Angel Maroni, were not based on truth. I had recently read two books that condemned Mormonism (we were in Mormon country) based on the same things that Dr. Shea had shared with me. I was surprised that a former Mormon would say these things about his childhood Faith, but I essentially also believed what Dr. Shea had said.

One Saturday morning, when I was home, I heard a quiet knock on the front door, and when I opened it, there was a young 11 or 12-year-old girl holding three tan-colored puppies, all about six weeks old and weaned. She said, "Would you like to have a puppy? They are free!" Well, I couldn't resist and picked out the one who was most calm and kept looking at me. This is how we got "Taffy," a wonderful family dog who stayed with us for over 14 years. When Luci came home that afternoon, she was very surprised but agreed that the children would like a dog. She grew to like Taffy even though she wasn't attracted to dogs as a young girl.

We were out West in cowboy country, so we purchased two rather tame horses, and we had many long rides with our neighbors in military housing, Mary Ellen and Andy Granuzzo. Andy was a Lieutenant Commander, a Navy helicopter pilot, and who eventually, after serving as Commander of a Helicopter Aircraft carrier, was made Admiral. I entered my Appaloosa horse, Candy, in a few horse shows, and won second place twice. I learned a lot about horses and their care during our time in Fallon. My other horse was a standard black horse who we named "Blackie" and was very gentle and was perfect for Luci.

I was invited and went deer hunting with about ten local ranchers in the mountains near Lovelock, Idaho in Northern Idaho. They brought along a full-time hired cook, and they had a special tent up set as a kitchen, saloon and poker den to cook and keep the "cowboy coffee" on

24/7. Cowboy coffee was strong regular coffee with no filter, grounds on the bottom, and raw eggs added for some reason which escaped me. It tasted fine, however. In the evening, after chow, it was time for poker games and drinking in the saloon. It was "party, party" every night, and lots of cowboy stories were told. We played Seven Card Stud in the tent until late at night. Everyone drank straight whisky out of the bottle. I couldn't do that. Too strong.

Some of them brought their own trailer to sleep in. Most of us slept under the stars. Our campsite was a Basque sheepherders camp. Proof of that was the sheep droppings all over the ground in this camp. It was used every Summer when the sheep were brought up to "high ground." It was so cold at night that I resisted getting up to go pee. I made sure that I slept on a slight incline of ground, so all I had to do was unzip my sleeping bag, and still laying there on my side, I could pee out, and the urine would run downhill away from me. We all hunted from horses.

I remember a Basque family (of retired Spanish sheep herders) dining place in Fallon (usually in a home} which served their food homestyle like "pass the potatoes." It was so good and reminded me of Grandma Anna's cooking.

I took my horse "Candy" hunting deer. We had to hobble the horses at night so they wouldn't run off with the many Mustangs in those mountains. My horse was only a few feet away from where I slept, and she was snorting all night long. I still slept well through that. One morning at Dawn, as we headed out to hunt, a herd of mustangs came galloping over a ridge right toward me, being chased by one of my hunting friends, and split off on both sides of me as they came running past. I noticed a mule in the herd with its long ears. All the horses had shiny coats as if they had been curried recently.

Another morning in the dark, we were riding along a very narrow goat trail, about a foot wide, around a mountainside when suddenly my horse Candy slipped and fell from under me. As I stepped off and she slid down the steep embankment. I didn't know what to do. Our leader said just wait and see what the horse will do. So sure enough, Candy was not hurt and came scratching and crawling up the Mountain, slipping and sliding, and came right up to me and was shaking like a wet puppy dog and acted as if I was the most important person in her life, she appeared glad to see me. Everyone got a mule deer on that hunt, and it was a great and fun experience. I started carrying a "Buck" knife after that experience because all the ranchers/cowboys on the hunting group carried one, and they always came in handy.

I made a lot of friends and enjoyed many social experiences with the residents of Fallon. Lots of Spanish Basque immigrants. One name that I remember was Ramone Arasabalaga, who owned a Basque-style restaurant. The locals, residents of Fallon had a Navy League Club, and every year had a big dance and invited the Navy. I never saw so many drunken cowboys and girls dancing, whooping it up, and dancing all night. I called it "Buckle Rubbing" when they danced because most of the men wore large belt buckles, and so did many of the women. A Western custom, I guess.

Luci and I were invited to go duck hunting on the local Indian Reservation with a senior Navy Commander at the base. As I drove to his house and entered his driveway, I could hear his blender going in the kitchen. He was making peach daiquiris! I knew then we were in for an interesting time and bird hunt. We, however, did get our limit of ducks and geese. You had to get a special permit to hunt on the reservation. One time during our hunt, the Commander, Luci, and I went into the water to get to a better cover to hunt from, but on the way to that place, the water turned to mud almost knee high.

Luci got stuck and used her shotgun like a cane to get out of the mud. We all had a laugh about that. The shotgun was not usable after that. I think Luci was OK with that. She didn't Like hunting or guns, but she was a good sport. Another time Luci and I went to a water well out in the middle of the desert which was used to test the distant water for radioactivity because the AEC was doing nuclear tests in Southern Nevada, miles away. It was, however, an excellent place for dove hunting because they would fly in for miles to get a drink of water and then roost on the wire fence. I and Luci each had a license, so we could harvest 24 doves in total. It didn't take long, and we had what we thought was our limit in our bag. We got back to our car, and a game warder was waiting for us and wanted to see our licenses, and the wanted to count our doves. So, I was confident and counted, "…22,23,24, whoops, 25." Just then, as I counted, the 25th dove and dropped it to the ground, it took off and flew away. I was amazed, and the game warden couldn't stop laughing. He said he had never seen anything like that in his life, me either. He sent us on our way. I know that God has a sense of humor, but this was too much!!

Luci's Chicken Posole recipe worked great with the 24 breasts of Dove. God is so good when you need Him, and He really does have a sense of humor!

Chapter 11

USS New Jersey (BB-62)

While still in Nevada, I read in the Navy Times that the Battleship New Jersey, BB-62, was being refitted to go back into service, primarily to the Viet Nam war. It sounded like a great adventure, so I applied. Commander Paul Farrell was to be the senior dental officer, and there were 11 dentists who applied for the number two position, but only one was to be chosen. Paul told me that he was allowed to look over the 11 records of the applicants, and he said that I was his choice because I had four children and was a Catholic.

Oh, again, God is so good!

Paul was born and raised "up the line" in Philadelphia and chose me because of my Catholic Faith as he was. The Ship was in the Philadelphia Naval Shipyard and would eventually be stationed in the South China Sea off the Coast of Viet Nam. In February 1968, I was assigned to the USS New Jersey BB-62. While outfitting the Ship in the Philadelphia Shipyard, my parents and Luci came for a short visit. We all stayed in a hotel room in the center of Philadelphia. We ate wonderful seafood every night fresh from the Chesapeake Bay. One night there were riots in the streets, and we wondered why? We found out that Martin Luther King had been assassinated that day. Needless to say, we stayed home that night and watched the rioting from our high-floor windows. Luci and my Mom, and Dad went back home to Minnesota, and I stayed. I went back to my little room in the BOQ. For the first time in my life, I was homesick. I called Luci one night, and we both cried on the phone.

During the months of refitting and renewing the New Jersey, I had time to roam around the Ship. I was already assigned my stateroom, which was a double with one set of bunk beds. I, however, didn't have to share it with anyone. I learned how to knot a MacNamera lace from one of the boson mates and lined the upper bunk bed safety bar with it. I also learned that my stateroom was the previous home of the Ship's head Supply Officer during WWII and had taken a direct hit during the night. I couldn't find out if he had died or survived the hit but I'm sure he didn't survive a direct hit. My stateroom had a teak wood deck above it, where the shell entered. I often heard the boson mates polishing the teak wood over my head with their broomsticks attached to the holy stone and swinging to-and-fro and chanting some sea-farers song as they cleaned and polished the teak.

During one of my wanderings around the Ship before the commissioning, I discovered that just one deck above me was "Admiral's Country." The door was not locked, and upon entry, I learned that the last occupant had been Admiral William "Bull" Halsey, who, during WWII, was the 3rd Fleet Admiral for the South Pacific, and the New Jersey was his "Flag Ship." He ruled over her and the 3rd fleet during many battles, including the Battle of Midway, which turned into one of the most decisive victories over the Japanese Navy and Land forces. He also attended the signing of the surrender of Japan on the USS Missouri, BB-63, on September 2, 1945, in Pearl Harbor, Hawaii. That battleship is now a museum and is still moored at Pearl Harbor and open to guests. I asked around the Wardroom (Officers Mess) about the history of Admiral Halsey's time in the New Jersey but didn't get a lot of information from anyone. His stateroom suite apparently was not used during the Korean War. The only usable piece of furniture in his quarters was a huge Leather lounge chair, which I could get down the ladder to my stateroom with much straining and grunting but which I enjoyed during my whole tour on the Ship. Thanks for your chair, Admiral!

After the shipyard was finished with refitting the ship we had sea trials to test everything except the 16 inch and 5-inch guns. After that I learned in the Ward-Room (Officer's Country) that the ship had passed successfully all trials and as a Navy tradition, a broom was hung from the yard arm to signify that the trials success was a "clean sweep."

After months of refitting and renewing, the Ship was considered seaworthy and ready for war. It was loaded with ammo and fuel, and food provisions, and we left the shipyard to go through the Panama Canal eventually and, after a stop in Long Beach, California and Pearl Harbor, Hawaii, and on to the South China Sea. After exiting the Panama locks, we anchored and had a "liberty call" in Balboa City. I was able to buy some fine lace tablecloths and bedspreads. A local lady hosted officers at her home for a fabulous dinner and entertainment.

We arrived and entered the South China Sea and commenced to do war on the Viet enemy immediately. For the many battle combat situations in which we were involved, I was assigned as Chief Medical Officer of the After Battle Dressing Station. I had hospital corpsmen, stretcher-bearers, an operating table, a big overhead surgery light, hull technicians to repair damaged bulkheads, and more. Fortunately, we had no causalities, and the Ship was never hit, in spite of exchanging a great deal of gunfire from enemy shore positions. During the many hours of downtime under "Zebra Conditions," I read the New Testament in the "Good News" Bible.

It was the restarting and a renewal of my spiritual education and learning more about Jesus and my Faith since I had become an adult.

Luci and I decided the best place for her and the children during this deployment was home in Faribault to live with good support from her parents and mine while I was gone. Before we got to Faribault, I called my Dad and told him to find an older house for us with three bedrooms. He sent us three options, and I chose one in a neighborhood that I was very familiar with. Just a few doors down from where my friend John Studer and Carroll Shaft lived. He made the down payment for us, and we headed home to look for the address of our new home. There we were: Luci and I in the car with four kids and a dog, Taffy, looking to see which house was ours. Everyone was excited. The girls had a bedroom together and the boys the same. It was a comfortable home even though I didn't spend much time there. Before I left for the ship, I built a small tree house in the tree in the back yard which I heard they enjoyed a lot.

One evening on the news after I was gone, Luci and a lady friend were watching Walter Cronkite on the news when he said that the New Jersey was hit by enemy shells and was sinking. Luci was in a panic. It was, however, not true; we were never hit. Does the news media ever get it right, even now after 50 years?

Vietnam

During the first day on the gun line off the coast of Vietnam, we were shooting at a big Viet Cong gun position far inland, and they were shooting at us. We had a Navy A6 jet airplane spotter who was giving us the position of the enemy guns, and we were firing rapidly from our 6" gun turrets. Finally, we had the target sighted and fired three rounds at once from our forward number one 16-inch turret and had a direct hit. The shelling from shore went silent, and our spotter relayed that we had made a direct hit. Unfortunately, his plane was also hit by ground fire and damaged, losing fuel, and he had to abandon his plane then he said over his intercom to our bridge, "Permission to come aboard, sir." In just a few minutes, his A6 appeared in the sky, and since we had an early warning from him, we had a lifeboat already in the water, and when he rough landed in the water next to us, he was easily rescued. I met him in the wardroom that night during dinner, and he was in great shape. That was some crazy first day on the "gun line in Vietnam."

Chapter 12

Emergency

A few weeks later, while still on the gun line, independently steaming up and down the coast supporting our troops with our 16-inch and 8-inch guns, I got a message from the Chaplain that my father was to have emergency brain surgery for a mass that showed up on x-rays, which eventually became a subdural hematoma. The Chaplain, who, by the way, was Catholic, asked if I wanted to go home. Since I was an only child and I knew my mother was worried.

I said, "Yes, I would go."

I took the next mail delivery helicopter and proceeded to help deliver mail to all the ships in the South China Sea until finally returning to an aircraft carrier. It turned out that I had to transfer to another carrier which would take me to the Clark Air Force base in the Philippines. We transferred at night and in the dark, in a two-propellor small plane, with heavy rain and wind. It took us three attempts to land on the carrier deck. That was very scary! I thought I was going to die.

Dear Lord, protect me! He did!

A day later, we headed for Clark Airforce Base in the same plane, and the pilot told me that when we arrived at Clark, he was only going to taxi on the runway, and I had to jump out, and I did. Another scary event!

Dear Lord, protect me again! He Did!

The next day I was on a flight to Okinawa, where I transferred again to a flight to Elmendorf, Alaska, where I was held up for two days. I finally got on a Medevac flight to Dover, Delaware. The long night flight was chaos at first because many of the injured vets had nightmares and flashbacks and were either crying or screaming for help.

A very young female Navy nurse was the only medical person escorting about 40 injured men and women. She came to me eventually and said there was much chaos, and she didn't know what to do. I told her to go, and I would join her and take their blood pressure one at a time and reassure them that everything would be all right and they were on their way home to get help. Don't worry about the blood pressure results just assure them and make sure you touch each of them physically. They are scared and alone and human touch is what they need. It worked, and the flight settled down.

I was totally exhausted and went back to sleep. From Dover, it took me two commercial flights to get to Rochester, Minnesota, home of the Mayo Clinic, and I found out that my Dad had successful surgery the morning before and was still in recovery. His hematoma was surgically and successfully removed, and he had a shaved head. I bought him a French barrette to cover his bald head, which he loved. I was jet lagged for 12 hours of time zones, so I had a difficult time adjusting. Luci had to feed me at midnight because I was wide awake and hungry. I stayed one week and took commercial flights from Minneapolis to Manila, Philippines, with many stops in between.

The flight attendants often upgraded me to First Class when available because I was in my only Khaki uniform.

When I inquired in Subic Bay on how to get to the battleship New Jersey, it was confusing because no one was sure day-by-day where the Ship was since it sailed independently up and down the Coast of Viet Nam supporting the ground fight, as I mentioned.

I decided to fly into Danang and see if I could get a helicopter ride to the Ship from there. No luck there. It was a little tense being in the country. Vietnamese people everywhere; they all looked the same, and I wasn't sure who the enemy was. I couldn't wait to leave. I returned to Subic Bay and eventually caught a mail delivery helicopter flight to New Jersey—a relief for sure.

Chapter 13

Navy in D.C.

My following assignment in 1968 was to the Naval Dental Clinic Anacostia in Washington, DC, in 1969. While I was there, one of my patients was Admiral Hyman Rickover, the Father of the Nuclear Navy as well as his wife, with a different dental appointment, the Chief of the Nursing Corp. His first wife had passed away a few years earlier. I do not remember her name. Maybe it was Admiral, when I had to talk to her. I do remember doing a root canal on one of her upper cupids.

Before I started treating Admiral Rickover, I tried to explain to him what I was about to do, and he said very gruffly, "Don't talk. Just do it!"

After I did the large filling for the Admiral on number 30, his lower right first molar, I asked him for a signed photograph for my memories of meeting him. He just looked at he and grunted. He said, "I don't have pictures and I don't do autographs."

The Master Chief, who was with him, looked at me and winked, and nodded his head. I received the photo a few days later. I think that photo is in my sea chest at my youngest daughter Sharon's house in Flagstaff, Arizona.

Beginning as Servant

While still at the Anacostia Dental Clinic, I discovered that my High School friend Phil Unser was stationed at the Naval Air Station Anacostia next to the Navy Yard where I was. He was the X.O. of the air base. He and I had gone down to the Navy recruiter in Faribault, our senior year in High School, and he surprised me by signing up, and I didn't. I went to pre-Dental and Dental School, and he went into the Navy as an enlisted man. Having his private flying license, he moved into the officer ranks soon, and by then was a lieutenant. When I finally went into the Navy after graduating from Dental School in 1963 as a Navy Lieutenant, Phil was a naval aviator and also a lieutenant.

We had lunch together one day, and I invited him to come to the clinic where I worked and to get some dental work done if he needed it. He came, and I replaced a lot of old fillings. During one session, he told me he was a light sleeper and often got up at 3 am to do paperwork, such as fitness reports, and usually drank most of quart of vodka starting in the morning before going to work and finishing it during the day surreptitiously. He didn't know that I had been trained as a Navy Drug and Alcohol counselor.

I told Phil that he was drinking excessively, and his health would suffer, and to think about his wife and children. I told him that I had a friend at the Naval Hospital in Bethesda, Maryland, who could help him slow down his drinking. I made an appointment, and Phil agreed to go. I told Phillip that I'll take you and introduce you to my friend. What I had really set up was what they called an "Encounter" where when Phil entered the room, His wife, daughter, his C.O., and a trained alcohol counselor were waiting for him.

After everyone in the room lovingly told Phil how his drinking affected their life together, his wife Helen said she was planning to divorce him if he kept drinking, and after he retired from the Navy, he would receive only half of his retirement pay and Helen would receive the other half due to divorce. He was mad as could be at me and everyone in the room, especially me, because I had tricked him into this Encounter. He got up to leave, and his C.O. ordered him to sit down and officially ordered him to enter the 6-month Alcohol Rehab Program at that Naval Hospital that same day. He had no choice.

After about 6 weeks of the program, Phil called me and asked me to go with him to an A.A. meeting outside the hospital which I agreed to do. I had hoped he was going to thank me and not kill me for how I had tricked him. Well, he thanked me, as did his two brothers, who were also in the Navy and who called me one evening at home. They both called me separately and thanked me for saving their brother's life. Phil retired soon after and moved to Pensacola, Florida, with wife and family. He got into real estate and eventually owned his own agency. He learned to play golf and was still sober by then, for life. We keep in contact. He retired recently, plays a lot of golf, and has many friends he and Helen socialize with. God bless you, Phil.

Chapter 14

More Education

One year later, in 1970, I reported to the Naval Dental School at the Naval Medical Center. In Bethesda, Maryland as a postgraduate student in General Dentistry. The program was very comprehensive. Covering all phases of dentistry and challenging. The curriculum included an all-year-long research study that we had to present for publication upon completion. I had a great research partner, Richard Esposito, and our project and research paper were accepted by the school and were eventually accepted for publication in a Professional Dental Journal of Endodontics.

In addition, at the end of the academic year, I received the award for excellence in Operative Dentistry. My name was etched on a brass plaque that hung at the entrance to the Naval Dental School in Bethesda, Maryland. Luci and I made many friends during that year, but eventually, we all went our separate ways and lost contact with them. My philosophy was "New places to go and new friends to meet."

My children didn't agree with me because they didn't like leaving their friends and schools but came along for the ride, and they made new friends again. I think, in the long run, it made them more rounded adults.

Chapter 15

Iowa

Following graduation from the Naval Dental Graduate Dental School, I requested and was assigned duty as a Graduate Student to the University of Iowa for two years, where I earned a master's degree in dental education. I really struggled with some of the courses, especially Statistics. I worked very hard and many long hours in the laboratory and the medical library on my research and thesis project. I also worked in the clinic assisting the students and advising and recommending treatment variations. Both my research project and my thesis passed unanimously during my Oral Exam, I was told by the head of the thesis committee, Dr. Johnson, who was also the head of the Operative Department, that my paper would have been acceptable for a Ph.D. because it was sound research and academically well-written. I called the research project and paper "The effects of Retentive pins on the strength of Composite Resin."

My theses was published in a Dental Journal, and my results totally contradicted a rather famous Operative dentist researcher from another University who claimed that retentive pins strengthened the composite resin. My testing and results showed the opposite and that retentive pins weakened the resin.

While still in Iowa, I volunteered to help the local Catholic Church Boy Scout troop to support my two sons. Ron Jr. was still a Cub Scout. We did a lot of camping, Summer and Winter. I remember waking up to a foot of snow on the ground and on the tent one winter morning. Surprise! Surprise!

I organized and planned a memorable trip to Northern Minnesota for a 7-day canoe trip for senior Boy Scouts. I required the scouts to achieve canoeing, camping, swimming, woodcraft, and hiking merit badges and the rank of 1st Class before they could go. Ten boys and 5 reasonably unfit adults took the canoe trip, which started in Ely, Minnesota. You had to be fit to portage the canoes and supplies over land. The adults got in shape during that week. It was a great adventure and experience both for the scouts and the adult men. One day we found a natural spring on a large Island, forming a small lake before it poured into the local river. I said to the scouts and adults, "Let's go skinny dipping!" They hesitated until I took off my clothes and jumped in. Then they couldn't get their clothes off fast enough and jump in too. The adults followed. It was great fun, and resulted in a lot of bonding of the boys to each other and the adults, who probably enjoyed the fun more than the boys. Every night we set up camp, pitched tents, built fires for cooking, and ate food that had been packed for us by Bill Rom's Outfitters in Ely.

The adults had one large tent to sleep in, and the boys had 4 tents, three to a tent. The adult men were all happy the first night when I pulled out a bottle of brandy to share as a night cap. We spread it out over 6 nights so it would last.

One day when we were canoeing a single file across a very large lake, a huge and rapidly moving squall came up with heavy winds and rain from the port side (left) of our canoes. I could immediately see that we were in trouble, and the waves that were forming would capsize the canoes shortly. I stood up in the lead canoe and shouted, "turn your canoes left and head into the wind." They all heard and did exactly as I said, and there were no overturned canoes, boys or men. That quick thinking, I believe, saved lives.

Thank you again, Lord!

The whole week was an exciting adventure that none of us will ever forget. The boys became men, and the men got in shape. We did it well, we did it safely, and we all got home in one piece. Good memories.

Chapter 16

Transition

During my second assignment to Great Lakes in 1973 as the Regional Director of Operative Dentistry, God began changing me even more. To be honest with you, that title didn't mean much to me because I was just one of the dentists on "the amalgam line." I had no other authority. During my lunch hour, I was often drawn to go to a small Catholic church which was locked during the day. I was able to get in through a cellar storm-door (remember them) and have the church all to myself. In that holy building, I'd sometimes prayed and/or slept.

One day, however, I received the "Gift of Tongues" and felt great joy but kept it to myself. I didn't even tell Luci. In the meantime, we were going to a Catholic church and I, as well as Luci and the children found the services to be very uninspiring especially the homilies. The priest wanted to talk more about his golf game and the money raising provided Bingo on Friday night. We started going to other churches in search of something but as we went from one church to another, we weren't sure what it was that we were in search of. Eventually, we ended up in an Evangelical Mission Church on a farm which was there mostly for alcoholics from Chicago and the place to dry out and to meet God. The people, both men and women were packed in and praying aloud in "tongues," prophesizing, singing and dancing in the aisles. I was attracted!

By all standards, it was a well-organized Evangelical church with an energetic head Pastor and a 5-piece band that blew the roof off. I had a bad cold and a stuffed nose and during the middle of the service was totally healed instantly. I only told Luci later.

Thank you, Jesus.

Luci and I and three of our four children (Debbie was not present) made an "Altar Call" at the end of the service. We spent three hours in that service and went back for three more hours in the evening, amazed, but never to return. *Why didn't we return?*

In my prayers, I told God I was a Catholic and needed to find a Catholic church where I could praise God as the Evangelicals did. Still, nothing happened. I was left high and dry. I attended a couple of Non-Catholic Charismatic prayer meetings, but I could not find whatever it was that I was in search of. For some reason or the other, it just did not feel right.

Then, one day driving home from work I told God that I was thinking about leaving the Catholic Church and joining a more charismatic church.

Immediately, I felt the words in my heart strongly state:

"Stay where you are, and I will send people to you. I want you to tell them about my Son."

I really didn't know what to expect.

I was happy to hear those words, but I still didn't have a church to call home. I eventually talked to a priest who suggested that I attend a charismatic prayer service at the Benedictine Monastery, in Bennet Lake, Wisconsin, just a few miles from my home in Petite Lake across the Minnesota-Wisconsin boarder.

The first evening, upon arriving, I found many Monks in the Chapel praying in tongues, praising God, prophesying and some dancing in the aisles. In that instance, I knew – I was finally at home. Two of the monks that I met at Bennet Lake were Fr. Michael Sawyer OSB and his nephew, Brother David Barfknecht, OSB who were eventually sent to Hawaii to establish a new Monastery in the hills near Waialua. My family and I started attending Sunday mass at the Bennet Lake monastery chapel and going out for brunch with Luci and the children after spending time after mass talking to some of the Monks. These brunches with only my family, were filled with jovial and good family time though one of my children, Debbie, said that, "I was a Jesus freak."

I wholeheartedly agreed with her! *Praise the Lord!*

Who did God send to me?

Many, and soon but it didn't stop then or there and continues to this day as I approach my 86ᵗʰ year.

Here are just two simple examples out of many:

One day, my dental Technician at Great Lakes was telling me that his life was going nowhere and that he didn't know what to do. I realized that he was a very intelligent young man who just needed a push in the right direction. We talked about God, and I suggested that he take some college classes in the local Junior College. He reluctantly said he would take one class, in which he got an "A."

To make a long story short, he excelled in college, left the Navy and went to dental school and came back into the Navy after graduation, and is now retired Commander. If I remember correctly, he is now in private practice and is a devout Catholic family man.

Another time still at Great Lakes, I started an Explorers Scout troop for those interested in dentistry. I noticed that a young boy was extremely interested in dentistry as a career. We started by talking about God and I told him that I considered the "healing of teeth" a ministry. He listened attentively and eventually I heard that he went to dental school. I lost track of him when I was transferred. Many more were to be sent to me and still are.

Children

While still stationed at Great Lakes, three of my children were in a Catholic school called Carmel High School. Debbie and Sharon were active in track and Field and Mike was doing great on the wrestling team. Ron Jr. was in a Catholic Grade school.

Debbie was always feeling sorry for injured animals and birds and would bring them home to care for them. She really loved animals and felt deep empathy especially for injured ones. A problem developed when she brought a young man home who was injured emotionally and was rotated in and out of various foster care homes. The young man's name was Pete, and people who tried to help him finally rejected him and he was moved from one foster home to another. Pete was very abusive to Debbie and would often rough her up, hit her and slam her against the wall. I witnessed one incident where he slammed her against the wall just inside of our home in the mud room. She didn't fight back.

Instead, she became resistant to our family rules and would often stay out until the wee hours of the night or not come home at all. Despite feeling discouraged, I loved her anyway. She stopped going to school and her and Pete slept in his car. She would talk disrespectfully to me and her mother and her siblings. I always got angry at Debbie when she said bad and disrespectful things to Luci. I felt like spanking her, but I could never catch her. Instead, I did what was in my power, and loved her anyway.

One night, the police from Chicago called me and said that they had Debbie in a cell.

"Do you want to come get her?"

"No." I answered firmly.

I thought this may wake her up to reality if she spent a night in jail. She came home the next day and announced that she was pregnant. It was now the middle of her senior year in High School. She stayed home to live with us, and Pete wasn't seen much anymore. One night, I went into her bedroom after she had gone to bed, and I prayed over the baby in her stomach.

I don't think she liked that but tolerated it and when I was done praying, she asked,

"Are you finished?"

"Yes," I answered, and she turned away from me.

It was alright. Despite her coldness, I loved her anyway. She was showing her pregnancy very early, and the school would not take her back because, they said, it was a poor example for the other children. She had also created a bad reputation of poor discipline and disrespectful responses to the school staff, as well as on the school bus toward other children. The school, Carmel High School, agreed that if she took two certain classes at the Local Community College, she would receive her High School diploma. She did that and got good grades. When her delivery time came, we took her to a nearby Catholic Hospital and I was told she had a rather easy delivery (just like Luci) of a beautiful baby girl. Apparently, an attorney in Chicago, who was representing a couple who wanted to adopt a child offered to pay for all medical expenses if that baby was given to them for adoption.

Debbie, Luci and I agreed, and the adoption process begun. The hospital stay was four days for Debbie and the baby, and during that time I was able to hold that "no name baby" every day. The day a Catholic Sister came and took the baby out of my arms, I cried my eyes out. Debbie had written a letter to the baby, as suggested by the attorney, and had asked the new parents through the attorney if the baby could be given the letter when she turned 18 years old. We went home with a huge void of sadness in our hearts. But still, I loved Debbie anyway.

I understand now why Debbie decided to find love and affection with women instead of men because of the mental and physical abuse she had received by Pete and others. I never believed she was a genetically born lesbian but was made this way because of the abuse she endured. Still, I believed that Debbie's motherly wishes led to have two more children without the burden of a male spouse. She had two more children from two different fathers, and she was a mom of three. She was a great mother, too. It had been a hard road for Debbie but now she is at peace, living with Christine, her youngest daughter, her husband Richard and two beautiful granddaughters.

One day I told Debbie, after Debbie's daughter was adopted and things had settled down, that what she was missing was "discipline" and that she could get that if she joined the Navy. Her response was,

"If the Navy has assholes like you in it, I will never go in."

Although her answer was cruel, I loved her anyway.

Surprise! Surprise! She did join the Navy and had a successful career and learned that she was very good with computers, the computer language, and how computers worked. She advanced quickly and became a senior chief in eleven years. It must be some kind of a record. She left the navy early at 11 years and stayed in the reserves until she retired and had a successful career in the civilian world of computers. I attended her "Hail and Farewell" party the day she left the Navy. I was so proud of her success in the Navy and in life.

Eventually, eighteen long years passed and the baby, Nancy, after reading the letter from Debbie, found us and came to visit us in Petite Lake, Illinois. When she entered our home, I held her for a long time and could only say the words, as I cried: "Oh, my baby."

Nancy met the whole family eventually and later met a nice man, Temmy Berkstresser, who loved her. They asked me to marry them which I did at their father's home deep in the forest in the hills of Tennessee. They had a beautiful home, and the ceremony was held in the forest of mature trees about which I commented looked like a huge green Cathedral. Temmy has great skills along with a vision and builds original boats for a living. His company is called "Berky Boats." They have two beautiful daughters named Mia and Luna and live in Florida where Temmy has his company. I wish we could see them more often, but distance stops us. I love them all, with all that I have in me.

Running for Health

With all of this going on while we lived at Petite Lake and I was working at Great lakes, I started running to release the effects of the day and to improve my health. I had been involved in athletics all my life and it seemed like a natural thing to do at my age. No membership, no team, no driving, just get out the door. I started running at noon during the work week in a triple basketball size gym, formally an airplane hangar, and did about two miles at a time. It made me feel so good. I also ran around the neighborhood at Petite Lakes and the fresh air made me feel even better. I met an army guy who was stationed at Fort Sheridan, and we started a challenge race between the Army and the Navy. The race started at Fort Sheridan and ended at Great lakes and was along the railroad tracks between the bases. It was close to 5 miles long. About twelve runners showed up and everyone enjoyed the race. The race was held way before any races were common and so it was a rarity. I don't think we had any prizes, except the promise of fun and accomplishment.

As I was transferred later to Pearl Harbor, Hawaii I joined a Sunday morning social running group at the Kapiolani Park Shell, which was run by a Dr. Jack Scaff, a cardiologist. He gave us instruction on how to run, how to be safe and how to train. It all lead up to the Honolulu marathon which was held the first Sunday of December. We started as a group running around Kapiolani Park which was about 4.5 miles in distance. Some of us started running around Diamond Head crater which was even further. Eventually a group formed of about 10 men and women who met at 6am at the shell and we ran to Hawaii Kai and back which was about the last 20 miles of the Honolulu Marathon route. When December rolled around, I felt that I was ready to try the 26-mile, 365-yard marathon.

I did alright and my time was 3 hours and 9 minutes. I was hooked and so were some of my friends and co-workers from the Pearl Harbor dental clinic. Dr. Hank Towle, a Periodontist, and I became running buddies and ran together after work and what we called an "adventure run" every Saturday morning. The adventure being to run in a different location every time. The best adventure was running the Diamond Head rim early one morning and stopping to overlook Waikiki and the ocean and mountain views. I ran all the Hawaiian Island's marathons, including Honolulu 3X, Maui 2X, Kauai, and the Big Island.

I was training 70 miles each week by then and this included hill running and track sprints. I qualified for the Boston Marathon by running the Honolulu Marathon in my first sub-3-hour marathon in 2:59:40. I also ran the New York marathon in just over 3 hours and ran with Ingomar Johannsson, the current heavy weight boxing Champion of the World for about the first 10 miles of the race until he petered out. I had my lowest time in the Marine Corps Marathon with a time of 2:56:10. I also ran the Maryland marathon, the London marathon and the Idaho Marathon. I ran 25 marathons in all, many 10 K races, half marathons and three Tin Man races which was approximately half of the Iron Man Held in Kona Hawaii annually. I quit keeping a log of my running after I went over 25,000 miles. I figured around the world at the equator was enough.

Today, at almost 86 years old, I walk a 1-2 mile course around my Condo complex daily except on Sunday. I also do floor exercises when I feel strong enough, to keep my upper body and core muscles toned up.

Our son Michael, for a while, adjusted to our move to Illinois better then Debbie. He was a freshman at Carmel High School. He was getting good grades (A's and B's) and was doing really well on the wrestling team. His coach was young and full of energy and wrestled with the team individually to show them techniques.

In Mike's sophomore year, his coach left for a higher paying job in a public school and was replaced by a very poor coach who didn't know much about coaching and was way over-weight. I could see that Mike was very discouraged, and almost immediately his grades took a dive and his enthusiasm dwindled. I think he was angry at this life change and began drinking excessively and illegally. I caught him trying to climb into his bedroom window one night after drinking in a boat on the lake and making so much noise that I couldn't sleep by my open window. He was also caught breaking into a neighbor's home and stealing some collectable coins. He was charged with theft and fortunately the judge made him promise to never steal again and put him on probation. I bought a beautiful restored, Chevy Impala for Mike to drive and give rides to Sharon and Ron Jr. to school. Within two months, he totaled it by running into a ditch after a night of drinking. In spite of these problems, I continued to encourage Mike and continued to love him. This time in Illinois was the hardest that I had ever experienced as a parent, and I often wondered how I had failed. I was told by many others that I should not blame myself for the wayward decisions of my children. Fortunately, Sharon and Ron Jr. were good children and never got into any serious trouble.

***

I planted a large garden on our terraced side yard. But after digging to overturn the soil I realized that about 2 inches down was solid clay. I ordered two truckloads of peat from a nearby bog. The rich soil was dumped in our driveway two levels above the garden area, so I had to take part of the rough-cut wooden fence and wheel barrel all of it down to the garden and spread it out.

It took all of one Saturday to accomplish, but now I had my garden with about 3 inches of peat soil as the top layer. I planted corn, peas, carrots, onions and green beans and did they grow fast. I attracted deer and raccoons almost immediately and had a constant battle with the hungry critters. One night I heard the garbage can get topped over and knew it was raccoons. I woke up Debbie and told her I needed her to hold a flashlight for me so I could shoot raccoons with my bow and arrow. Her eyes lit up with excitement. I knew if we ran out to the garbage can area, we would surprise them and they would run up the oak tree next to the garage, and they did. I aimed the light up at them and there were 4 shiny eyes looking down on us. I had a direct hit with each arrow and the raccoons came tumbling down at us. Debbie was impressed and I was happy to rid of two garden raiders.

***

We had purchased a large home with a full basement and two floors above right on the shore of Petite Lake one the smallest lakes of the five "Chain of Lakes." I bought a speed boat for water skiing and a small 12-foot plastic/Styrofoam sailing boat which we used a lot every Summer. We also had to put in a long dock every spring and had to take it out before the lake froze over with ice in the Winter. Only a young and strong man could get that done twice every year. All the Chain of Lakes were connected by channels and that gave us the opportunity to take friends out to dinner in our boat and to just go cruising around the other lakes. We had fore and aft lights on our boat and a search light to help guide us through the channels.

The largest Lake was named French Lake and had many large sleeper yachts present and often in the daytime or all night. They were often tied up to each other, and I would see five or more Yachts together in the middle of the lake with very loud and boisterous parties going on day and night. It looked like fun. Our dog Taffy liked to explore and often would go to the land next to our channel and chase muskrats.

One time I saw her swimming back toward our dock when she suddenly cried out "yelp" and went under the water for a couple of seconds. She got to shore and ran up to our house and upon inspection I noticed she had been bitten on the neck, and was bleeding. I figured that she was probably bitten by an angry muskrat. She eventually healed without any medical care necessary. She broke her right front leg another time when the back door slammed shut on her leg caused by one of our teenagers who was not observant and was careless. She had a cast on her leg but fortunately healed quickly.

Chapter 17

Hawaii

We were transferred next to the Navy Regional Dental Center at Pearl Harbor, Hawaii. Almost immediately afterwards, God started sending people to me who had various needs. Many more were to come because of our trip to Medjugoria, Yugoslavia in 1979. Prior to going to Medjugoria, I was attending daily mass at St. Peter and St. Paul churches in the Ala Moana before going to work. Before mass, I usually sat on the far-left side in a pew just below a statue of Mary. I prayed to Mother Mary for protection and to have a good and safe day at work. Eventually, a very specific prayer formed in my heart, and I recited it every day. I told Luci about this prayer, and she said,

"You should write it down, because it is so good".

I took her advice and wrote it down, and I called it "Daily Prayer to Our Mother Mary." I recorded these words:

"Mother Mary, I come to you as your child, knowing that your arms are open. I ask you to enter my unworthy heart. Secure there a home familiar to Jesus, because of your presence, and prepare for Him a throne from where He will rule my life as Lord and King. Mother Mary, I consecrate myself to you today, and give you all of myself: my body, soul and my humanity. I also give you all my thoughts, words and actions so that you may dispose of them for the most perfect intention. I pray for the souls in Purgatory, the men and women religious and clergy of the Church, and for my family. Mother Mary, protect me from the evil one and lead me to Jesus, and your Spouse the Holy Spirit, so that one day I well be able to join with all in Heaven, giving praise and worship to the Father. Amen.

Over the years, as Luci and I traveled all over the world, I left many copies of this prayer in churches whenever it was possible. I estimated that the number of prayer cards distributed were somewhere around 10,000. God didn't say "Tell them about My Mother," but I did.

***

We arrived in Medjugorje on Christmas Eve and stayed with a family that Fr. Michael Sawyer had stayed with on a previous trip he had made, and we were welcomed with open arms as part of the family. We went immediately to St. James church after settling in and getting something to eat, to Midnight Mass because it was Christmas Eve. Upon arriving, we saw a huge crowd surrounding the front of Saint James church who could not get in because it was packed with people in the pews and had standing room only. They had loudspeakers outside of the church, so we stayed to hear the Midnight Mass.

I noticed two things that I thought were unusual during the mass: First, even though it was winter, with snow on the ground, we did not feel cold. Second, between the two bell towers of St James church was a brilliant and extra bright star which did not change position during the 2-hour mass. We were very touched by these revelations, and we decided to go to mass again on Christmas Sunday morning so we could worship inside. We went two hours early to Mass the next morning in order to get a seat. We entered an empty church and took our place in the front row. I told Luci that I was going into the Sacristy where there had been recent apparitions of the Blessed Mother to the children of that village.

As I entered the Sacristy, I observed a statue of who I thought was St. Joseph on my far right and a statue of Mary in the opposite corner. I went to Mary and knelt to pray. I closed my eyes and immediately a vision appeared in my mind of a tunnel with a light in the far opening. I could see people moving at the end in the light, but they were not clear as if a lace cloth or veil was at the end of the tunnel between them and me. I imagined that this was like the tunnel that people experienced during death going toward Jesus, the light however, was not moving and neither was I. Then the words came to me:

"Do something about abortion."

I knelt for a while wondering what I could do about abortion. I finally opened my eyes, and the vision was gone, and with it, the "statue" of St Joseph had also disappeared. I got back to the front pew and told Luci what happened and then felt something happen in my pocket. I needed to look. I drew out my rosary which had been a gift from my mother to her father and which I had seen in his clasped hands in his coffin at his funeral mass just two weeks before in Minnesota. I asked my mother if I could have the rosary and she took it from his cold hands and gave it to me. After withdrawing it from my pocket I noticed that the corpus of Jesus on the cross had turned to the color of gold. Also, the chain links between the prayer beads had turned to gold. The people we were staying with said it was a miracle and a message to me. I asked one of the priests at the church (St James) what the message *"Do something about abortion,"* meant and he didn't know but suggested to just "wait for more information." Strange answer, I thought.

As a side note: a nurse friend of Luci, Lucille James, from Honolulu had also come to Medjugorje at the same time. She told us that she had gone up the small mountain in Medjugorje with friends. While we were there, to pray at the huge cross which was situated on the peak of the mountain. We were there at the same time and left before sunset. She told us that she and her friends stayed until it got dark and were afraid to go down the mountain because it was dark, cold and steep. She noticed a guard in a small room with a light on, at the base of the cross, so her and others she was with felt safe and stayed the night to pray. She didn't feel cold during the night. In the dark of the night, she was given the gift of the sound of the rosary being prayed in the whole world, all at the same time. She said is sounded like the ocean and the waves coming in and out from the shore. She eventually fell asleep. She woke refreshed and started down the mountain and noticed that there was no guard and no small lit room at the base of the cross, just solid concrete.

After the Medjugorje trip, Luci went back to Great Lakes because she had to attend school, and I went to Fort Lauderdale, Florida to visit my parents who spent the winter there. Our friend Audrey Ward also went back to North Chicago to her home and told us she was now saying the rosary daily because of her experience in Medjugorje. I had one month leave from the Navy. I told my mother everything that had happened, and I suggested that we say the rosary together as a family, which we had not done ever before. We asked my father to come in the room to pray with us. My mother had bought 3 identical rosaries at a retreat, years before when she was very young; one that I now had which she had given to her father; one for my father which he held and one for her. We said the rosary, but my father couldn't say his part because he couldn't stop crying. After praying, my father left the room and my mother noticed immediately that her rosary had turned gold just like mine. We compared our rosaries and talked a lot about the meaning of the changes in our beads being a gift and why our rosaries had changed. We decided that God was giving us a sign that He approved of our family praying together and that we should continue praying together if possible. My Mother said she wasn't sure if my dad would pray with her, but still, she was hopeful. I told her that Luci and I were already praying together.

God is aware of us and blessing our family prayers!

Chapter 18

Benedictines

Luci and I were transferred in 1976 to Hawaii. I was assigned to the Navy Dental Clinic at Pearl Harbor. We eventually met up with Father Michael Sawyer and Brother David Barfknecht, whom we knew at the Monastery at Bennet Lake, Wisconsin. They had established a Monastery in the hills above Waialua on the North Shore of Oahu. They also brought a Catholic Sister MaryJo MacInneny who helped establish the monastery in 1983. Brother John Kudia also was with the original group. Sister MaryJo had attended a counselor training class recently concerning post-abortion emotional damage to women and men. The training program was called '*Hope Alive*' and a book titled "Deeply Damaged" was used in the training program. The program was being conducted in Victoria, British Columbia, Canada, at a location called "Mount Joy College" and suggested we go to this training.

"Do something about abortion."

We went soon after and after 80 hours of intensive training in 7 days conducted by Dr. Philip Ney Md, Ph.D. (Psychology) and founder of *Hope Alive* and his wife Dr. Marie Ney, originally from France, we were ready to serve God's wounded people, but first we were asked by Dr. Ney to help him train other counselors. That put us around the world not only training in Vancouver, British Columbia, and Canada but also in Singapore, Kenya, Africa, Oxford, England, County Carlow, Ireland, Strasburg, France, L'viv, Ukraine, Manilla, Philippines and Hawaii, and on the United States mainland. Each training weeklong session included the framework of the counseling program as the training tool so that the trainees experienced not only the learning process but also the healing of the wounds from abortion. Many of the trainees had experienced at least one abortion and/or had a friend or relative who had an abortion.

While Luci and I were visiting at the Monastery in Wailua, Hawaii one day I was spending a lot of time talking to a visiting priest who was on retreat who was from Minnesota. I noticed that Luci had been talking to a married couple for a long time, and she had a concerned expression on her face. My priest friend told me that he thought my aloha shirt was exceptionally beautiful and was admiring it. When we got home, I washed and ironed the shirt he liked and sent it back to him in Minnesota with a short note. He wrote back later and said,

"You never know when someone is going to give you the shirt off his back."

It was a very nice note that he sent, and his gratitude was genuinely described.

A few days later, I came home and went into our walk-in closet and noticed that there were a lot of my clothes missing. I asked Luci about my clothes, and she answered,

"Remember that couple I was talking to at the Monastery the other day? Well, they were very poor and were forced to move back to the mainland because he could not find work in Hawaii and he didn't have many clothes to wear to go on job interviews. So, I gave him a bunch of your clothes, including a suit, shirts, pants, a pair of shoes, underwear, socks, etc., and put them all in our new suitcase so they could get them home."

I was surprised, but then thought of the priest from Minnesota and the shirt I gave Him and figured that God, in His humor, said to give more, not less to those in need.

My heart smiled and I knew that Luci did the right thing.

***

While still in Hawaii I attended a Good Friday Rite at St. John Vianney church in Kailua, Hawaii. During that event, we were given the opportunity to venerate the cross up in front near the altar and kiss the cross if we chose to do so. I got in line, and it was long, so I had time to pray. I thanked Jesus for his sacrifice of death on the cross and I prayed that I could serve Him in some way and how could I do that? Before I got halfway to the cross, I heard these words,

"Be like her. Be kind and be simple."

I looked up and immediately saw Sister Rose Daniel, an elderly Maryknoll Sister leaving the cross and walking to her left. I had gotten to know her when one day we visited their home on the beach in Lanikai. The plumber had just left after fixing a leaky pipe under the sink and the whole kitchen floor was a mess, so I got a bucket of soapy water and cleaned the floor. I also knew Sister Rose from a Charismatic Prayer group that I led for a while until we moved back to Honolulu. Those words "Be like her" have stayed with me all of my life, right to this day, even at this present moment.

Chapter 19

Philippines

In the Philippines, we had our International Hope Alive Meeting at a resort owned by a famous Philopena singer, diva, and actress named Ku Ludisima. The international group we were attending went by the name IHACA (International Hope Alive Counseling Association.) The program Hope Alive was, at this point, being conducted in about 30 different countries. The training/counseling and the exchange of experiences was always worth the trip. My friend Michael Masumbay from Uganda, Africa also came to the conference. He ran an orphanage for children orphaned from the AIDS epidemic in Africa.

He brought handmade cards and envelopes to the conference made by the orphan children from a machine that I had purchased for him. They were made from scraps of paper disposed of in the trash by others in the town nearby. The paper was washed, bleached and ironed flat and dried in the sun and made into cards with African designs and envelopes. Michael brought hundreds of the cards and envelopes, and he wanted to sell them to the conference members to make money for the orphanage. He asked me how much to charge for packets of 10 cards and envelopes and how should he sell them? I told him to make a sign that said "Made by My Orphan Children. Donations only."

Well, that worked. Michael sold all of them and he said he got triple the amount of money that he expected.

I had earlier given Michael money for a generator so they could have lights at night. He said that when he had the generator hooked up for electricity, he brought all the children into the main gathering room (refectory) and told one of the older kids to flip the switch and when the lights went on the kids jumped and screamed and danced for joy, because they had light for the first time. I later went with Michael to the small village near our meeting place which had a swap meet in progress so he could buy shoes for himself and his wife. He bought two pair of shoes for his wife and one pair for himself. He then started to look at watches but the cheapest one was more then he could afford. When we got back to the resort, I gave him my watch. We are now friends for life.

Accident

One morning in our cabin at the conference, I was sitting on the bed preparing for a talk that I was to give that afternoon while Luci was taking a shower. The shower was not enclosed but just a corner of the bedroom with a short curb to keep the water from going into the room and could drain into the corner drain. I heard Luci yelp and then heard her fall and a "crack" sound as she slipped and fell and hit the back of her head on the curb. She started bleeding excessively and was unconscious but woke up quickly. I grabbed a towel and put pressure on her large cut and called for help. I discovered after we were waiting for the ambulance to come that the tile used in the shower area was the same tile as on the walls and was a very slippery, shiny surface which obviously would not hold a foot from slipping like regular shower tiles would have.

An ambulance took her and me to a small country style clinic where her head injury was cleaned and stitched. She was then taken again by ambulance into the main hospital in Manila, Makati Medical Center, where x-rays showed a skull fracture in Luci's right occipital skull bone in the back of her head. The hospital was a far cry from American hospitals, but she was attended by a Neurologist who came to check on Luci daily and did many tests. His concern was that Luci's brain was swelling which could be fatal and he planned to do an intracranial drain or shunt the following Monday morning.

Upon arrival that morning, the doctor noted, after tests, that Luci's brain swelling was reduced, and he decided to observe her progress for a few days. *Thank you, Jesus!* She was still not "out of the woods" and most of the day and night she would drift in and out of consciousness. There were no nurses on duty at night so I had to hire two nurses to stay with Luci so I could go home to rest. Home was a large compound owned by Ku Ludisima, who part of a singing group called "The Three Divas." They entertained locally and in various countries around the world. Also present in the compound was her ailing mother who was on hospice watch by rotating nurses and had 24-hour care and attention. Ku had multiple buildings walled in with a 12-foot cement walls surrounding the compound. She had 3 cars, a chauffeur, a cook, gardeners, and others doing various duties including an armed guard at the only gate to enter or exit the compound. She also had one man that all he did was make her fine jewelry which she wore during her singing engagements. She didn't like to wear the same jewelry twice. What a Diva!!

I lived in the main house with Ku and her daughter, Julianna. I was told her husband was in prison for murder. I didn't ask any questions. Ku told me that I didn't have to worry about the medical expenses for Luci because she would pay all of them. Although she had said that she totally failed to produce any money toward Luci's medical costs when the bill came. I got a ride with her chauffeur to the hospital, whom she fired, while I was there because he had a cough, and she was afraid he had tuberculosis which might spread to her and her family and employees. He drove me into the hospital every morning and I took a cab home in the evenings. A man who I knew from the resort contacted me and we met for lunch one day. He told me that one of the cooks at the resort had an accident and was burned seriously due to a kitchen fire. He was taken to the hospital and built up a lot of medical expenses, which Ku said she would pay for, but she never did. He did not survive his burns and died soon after being admitted to the hospital. My friend warned me that Ku would do the same thing concerning Luci's medical expenses. He was right. One good thing about the hospital is that it was Catholic and it had a large beautiful Catholic chapel on the top floor and had daily mass every noon, which I attended. I also took a long power walk every day while Luci was sleeping which included going up and down the subway stairs and across to the next street to stay in shape. I was told that the main street in Manila, which went right in front of the hospital, had previously been an American airplane runway constructed by the American Seabees after the Japanese were driven out of the Philippines. There was also a park in the center of town with a large pagoda where noon mass was held seven days a week on an open air sanctuary. I went to mass there a couple of times for a change of pace. Thousands of local working people attended mass there daily. The people have a deep faith, and they openly express it.

Every time I went out on the street young boys would approach me for money with big sad but eager eyes. I always had change in my pocket so I would flip a coin high into the air and while they were scrambling to get the coin, I would disappear.

After one month Luci was discharged to go home to the Rehab Hospital of the Pacific in Honolulu by medevac. I inquired about the hospital bill and the medevac cost. I was shocked to learn that I had to pay the medevac fee in advance and the total cost, Manila Hospital and medevac was $60,000.00 USD. I had to call Visa and explain my situation to them and thankfully Visa extended my line of credit to cover these bills. When I got home to Hawaii, I had to sell my complete 12 extra fine American gold coin collection at a loss, to pay off my Visa bill. Luckily, I can say that it was all worth it for Luci. The flight back to Hawaii took 6 seats of space which were replaced by a stretcher type bed which Luci was strapped to for the whole flight. They hung a curtain all around her area, so she had privacy. She was accompanied by a nurse and nurse-aid on the flight. My seat was next to Luci's space. She was not conscious during most of the whole 8-hour flight as far as I could tell. She was however, awake on and off and so I was able to talk to her for short spans of time to remind her that I was with her and had a seat next to her. She had to spend another 4 weeks in the Rehab Hospital in Honolulu before she was strong enough to go home. What an ordeal.

Thank you, Lord, for the strength and calm mind to withstand this test.

Chapter 20

Encounters

I remember one Lady in our first training/counseling session in British Columbia, Canada who I had in a group of four counselees. This particular woman was troubled about her identity. She looked like an American Indian to me and stated that she thought she was part American Indian but had no proof and no Indian family that she knew of.

This woman suspected that she was adopted but was never told about it. In the time that our paths crossed, she was married and had two daughters. One morning, she told me and the group about a dream that she had that previous night. As part of her assignment, she had also drawn a picture of the dream. She described that she saw a large house and front porch with her family all standing on the porch watching her chasing a large bear around in a circle.

As she narrated the events of her dream, she mentioned how she wasn't sure if she was chasing the bear or if the bear was chasing her. Sometimes, they reversed direction. No matter what she did in the dream, the woman just couldn't catch up to it. When the bear turned and chased her, it never caught her either. Just then, it came to me to tell her this story: She was in body, heart, and soul a an American Indian and her name was "Running Bear." She was totally in awe at my suggestion of her Indian name and race. She cried and laughed and was totally struck by the idea and translation of her dream.

Her family was not aware of her many years of fretting over who she was, so they just stood (in the dream) on the porch of the house as passive individuals, and just observed. The woman could now identify herself and an Indian woman and was assured of her identity as a Squaw Mother of two daughters, who now could be comfortable living in the white man's world because she now was at peace knowing who she was. Eventually, the truth was brought out into the open— her adoptive parents had kept that information from her thinking to protect her.

She forgave her adoptive parents for not telling her that she was adopted. At the end of the week, the counselees were given the day off to go shopping in Victoria town and she found a picture of a beautiful and young Indian Mother with an eagle feather in her hair, dressed in Indian leather clothes with leather laces hanging from the sleeves and decorative beads around her neck and wrists, with her two daughters sitting beside her dressed also in Indian clothes like their mother. She bought the framed photo and presented it to me the next day as a gift and with tears in her eyes expressed her thanks to helping her discover who she was.

That framed photo was a special gift from her to me during the *Hope Alive* week of training/counseling. I have treasured it all these years. She signed it, "With Love, Running Bear."

I could never forget this week, for the rest of my days. Similar to this woman's awe-inspiring tale, many other stories touched our hearts like this during our world travels doing *Hope Alive* training/counseling. I will go Country to Country describing the most important and memorable events relayed by the trainees/counselees in the succeeding chapters.

I'll send people to you.

Chapter 21

Ukraine

Our week in Ukraine also produced many stories. We did our training in a city named L'viv in the Northern part of the country, about 90 miles Southwest of Warsaw Poland. We were met at the airport by security guards who all carried Uzi Machine guns and didn't look like they wanted our presence or were happy to have visitors to their country.

We spent our time far from the main city and conducted our training/counseling in a small rundown hotel right near the exit of the airport. I noticed that, despite the poor condition of the Hotel, there were many luxury cars like Mercedes, Bentleys and BMWs parked in front of the hotel. I learned later that the Mafia had daily meetings in the hotel. Each floor of the hotel had a guard posted near the stairway (no elevator) who also didn't seem to approve of our presence. My bed had broken springs in it and I didn't sleep well most nights. Luci's bed, on the other hand, was just okay.

There were two Irish counselors with us and 3 Irish trainees. Every night they gathered in a room across from Luci and I and were singing Irish songs very loud and boisterously. I went over the second night to check them out and thinking there would be a lot of beer drinking to go with the singing, only to discover there was no alcohol, just happy Irish lads and lassies singing their favorite ditties.

A most memorable experience in L'viv was with a family of a mother and her two daughters, who were all three Licensed OBGYN doctors and practicing. The mother admitted to doing at least 500 abortions while the two daughters were forced to do two abortions during their residency but had not done an abortion since graduation and starting their own OBGYN practice. They could both not bear the thought of killing an unborn baby.

During one of the sessions, one of the daughters excused herself to go to the bathroom. While she was gone, the remaining sister began to tell how she always had the feeling that there was a spirit who was trying to reach her. She felt this was a friendly spirit and that this spirit was always with her. She became so used to the spirit that she finally named her 'Maria.' She knew that this was a spirit or person who was somehow "missing." She also said that she never told her sister of this spirit or the fact that she had named her Maria.

Shortly after sharing this story, her sister returned from the bathroom and joined the group next to her. Dr Ney began to ask this second sister if she had ever felt like there was someone missing in her life. She said yes, there was a friendly spirit who was constantly with her, and she also admitted that she had never mentioned these feelings, of experiencing this missing spirit, with her sister in their lifetime and that she had named her Maria.

Well, you can imagine that the two sisters who had not shared their secret with each other about third sister and had both named the missing spirit Maria began to sob tears of joy and discovery. They also quickly privately asked their mother if she had aborted a child and if the fetus was a girl. The mother, now also in tears said yes. Their family was whole again.

Now the mother who had kept this abortion of a girl fetus a secret for thirty years began to sob tears of sorrow and relief. The three of them held each other and cried their eyes out now finally having the truth come forward. The healing of this family was miraculous and wonderful. Dr. Ney had to end the session because everyone started crying, including Luci and me. After this experience and many other similar experiences, we learned the true power of the *Hope Alive* program and its healing effects.

God is so good!!

Chapter 22

Ireland

In the same vein as these experiences, another event occurred when we were training/counseling people in County Carlow, Ireland. We conducted the training in a country estate in what was called the "Rathvinden House.' It was a huge estate or manor of about 50 acres and had a 5-bedroom guest house, horse stables, and gardens and large fields for horses to run on and feast on the grass.

The main manor house had 12 bedrooms, and several parlors with fireplaces, a well-stocked library and a dining room which had a table that easily seated 20 people. The kitchen was as large as any restaurant would have. A friendly but sad looking Irish Hound as big as a Great Dane sat at the side door waiting to get in, but that never happened. Six of the young ladies who were to take the training/counseling were already in residence. We were informed that this estate was previously owned by C.S. Lewis, the famous author of many novels including "Narnia" which became a Hollywood movie. Now, however, the estate was owned by Douglas Gresham, who was one of C.S. Lewis's two adopted sons through Joy Davidman who Lewis met through mail correspondence concerning a mutual love of Literature composition. They eventually married and Lewis adopted the two sons after the wedding.

While we were here, we also got to visit C.S. Lewis's home in Oxford, England before he married, called the "Brick House" because it was located across from a brick foundry. Of course, it was constructed from the bricks produced by that factory.

Our group of 4 trainers, including Dr. Ney, assisted in the training of 12 English and Irish trainees. Douglas Gresham and his wife Merrie were our hosts. Douglas looked like a character right out of a Sherlock Holmes or Abby Lane with his white turtleneck sweater, blue blazer, riding boots, horse whip and his well-kept Van Dyke mustache. This is how he presented himself every day. Merrie Gresham, his wife, gave me a solid brass shoehorn that she noticed I was admiring just before we left. She was an exceptional hostess.

Many years later, we visited the Gresham's in their new home in the Island country of Malta.

Chapter 23

Kenya

In Nairobi, Kenya, we did our training in a large convent run by Italian nuns and a few African women/girl recruits who were in various stages of their commitment to the religious life. The compound containing the convent was surrounded by a 12-foot-high stone fence topped with broken glass imbedded in the cement on top of the wall. It had a gate that was manned by an armed guard who would not let anyone unauthorized enter. While we were there, two car jackings occurred during which the driver who had stopped to look was shot in the head and tossed into the ditch as his car was stolen and taken away. We felt completely safe inside the walls of the convent despite the dangers that lurked outside. The sisters were very hospitable and gracious in welcoming us as well as feeding us and providing us with small, but extremely clean private rooms to sleep in. Each bed was furnished with a mosquito netting to prevent insects with malaria's potential venom from biting us. Mass every morning was filled with beautiful African chanting, along with drumming with a sort of jungle drum and with a deep rhythmic boom.

One night I heard Luci moaning, and I asked her if she was sick. She answered that she had a bad headache, so I got up and got her a pain pill and a glass of water. We both went back to sleep. In the morning when we were walking to mass, Luci was dragging her left foot. I knew then that her headache had been a cranial stroke. It turns out she had two strokes, one on the left and the other on the right side of her brain. She completed the training with me as the counsel leader without saying anything. I knew she was sick but didn't know how serious it was. As a precaution I found out that the American Embassy had a resident physician. I called them and found that the physician was traveling and would not return to Kenya for a few weeks. As disappointing as that was, they told me to check Luci into the emergency room at the Kenya hospital.

Since it was night-time by now, we were able to get a ride to the main city by an employee of the convent and get checked into a "Pensione," owned and run by another Catholic Sister group. We were given a small room with one small bed. The trip through the city that night was filled with black men poorly dressed and who all looked desperate and dangerous. I found out later that unemployment in the city was 40%. No wonder there were men and boys wandering around in the night looking for trouble. I contacted the American Embassy again just in case he or she came back early and was told that he was still out of the country and that he wasn't sure when he would return.

The next morning, we took a taxi (filthy dirty with cracked leather seat covers and trash on the floor) to the hospital and checked Luci into the Emergency Room. Describing this hospital is particularly difficult because never had I ever been in a hospital which was in such a decrepit state; completely tattered and run-down and it was like something in a movie during the 1930's in a third world country. Everything was dirty and unhygienic, and the equipment appeared to be outdated.

There was trash in the hallways. light bulbs hanging from cloth coated wires from the ceiling and bed sheets stained with old filth, as well as water dripping from faucets into rusty sinks, and there were no towels, either.

Black people looked at us with wide eyes, probably wondering what we were doing there. I had the same thoughts. The exam in the ER was brief and we were told that we had to wait for the doctor who would come some time the next morning. I had to leave Luci there to return to the Pensione to retrieve our luggage and personal belongings because I didn't feel it was safe overnight. I retrieved our luggage and walked back about a mile to the hospital because of the ridiculous charge we had paid for out last cab ride. (A rip off.) It was a scary walk and all I could do was ask God to protect me. I arrived unharmed and spent the night on the floor in Luci's hospital room. I learned that most patients were fed by their family who would bring food to the hospital every day. A doctor finally came in the afternoon and suggested we go back to the U.S. to get treatment. By then Luci was feeling better and we were given a ride to the airport by a hospital staff member arranged by the doctor.

After that, we couldn't get out of Africa fast enough.

Almost Got Home

It took us three days to get to Los Angeles and we finally had a good night's sleep. The next morning, however, Luci was totally uncoordinated and was slipping out of bed trying to get up until I grabbed her to prevent her from falling to the floor. I knew then that we couldn't go on toward home in Hawaii. I decided to call a friend, Pat Warren who had been in my Hope Alive International training in Hawaii. He held a PhD in Religious Studies and was a teacher and professor in a Catholic Priest formation Seminary in Oxnard, California. I told him, the situation with Luci and he said, "Stay where you are, and I'll come to get you."

He arrived about 6 hours later and was an answer to our prayers. *Oh, Thank, you God.* Pat made sure that we were fed first and he drove us directly to his home in Oxnard after about a three-hour drive. During our lunch, Arnold Schwarzenegger came dashing in with a large group of followers. I was told that he headed for an auditorium in the hotel where he was to give a speech as he was running for governor of California.

The next morning, after staying at Pat's house, Pat called a doctor friend who suggested a vascular surgeon in Oxnard who was respected and known throughout the area as the best vascular surgeon to contact, which we did. His secretary arranged for Luci to be seen the same day at 1pm and Pat gave us a ride to the doctor's office. The first thing the doctor did was take X-rays of Luci's internal carotid arteries and then sat us down and said to Luci, "You, are lucky to be alive young lady. After looking at the images of your internal carotid arteries, I see that they are both 90% blocked. You must have surgery ASAP."

His plan was to do one side at a time which he did starting the next day. Luci recovered and one week later he did surgery on the other side. During this time, I stayed with Pat and his wife who was a writer and poet. She hardly connected with me during my 3 weeks stay. She was sort of a recluse. Every morning Pat would get up at 5 am and after sounding a small gong in his living room, would meditate for one hour. I joined him and found it to be a very healing and a peaceful encounter with God especially since I was experiencing such a stressful time. Following meditation, we would go for a 5 mile walk in the cool fresh air (at least in Oxnard it was cool) of central California. After he prepared breakfast for us (his wife always slept late), he would drop me off at the hospital with the promise to pick me up at 5:30 pm. Pat always prepared dinner from a health food store, so it was very fresh, nutritious and healthy. His wife did not eat with us. After the second week of recovery, Luci had two sessions a day in rehab for about ten days, where she did very well and recovered quickly.

Three weeks later, Pat was dropping us off at LAX for a flight back home to Hawaii. It's hard to believe that there are friends who are so willing to go all the way to help us when we are in need.

God is so good! Again, and again!

Pat died of a major stroke a couple of years later and I'm sure he is waiting for us to join him in Heaven someday.

Goodbye Pat and thank you for your friendship and hospitality. *You are really a Saint now*!

Chapter 24

Singapore

Our trip to Singapore was very educational and exciting. Dr. John Seah and his wife came with us and acted as our guide and host. He was born and raised in Singapore and trained in Ireland where he met his wife, Katherine, a full-blooded Irish lady. What a combination!! Again, we stayed and conducted our training/treatment sessions in a convent of Chinese nuns. One young lady of the group, that I was the leader of, told a story about her brother who had committed suicide by jumping off a tall building.

God, please forgive him and bring him to experience eternal joy in Your Kingdom.

On the first anniversary of his death, she was drawn to the building roof where her brother had jumped from. While she had her eyes closed, she heard her brother's voice thanking her for coming and telling her that he missed her. She started to cry. He then told her that she could join him if she jumped of the building as he had done.

He begged and encouraged her to jump. She opened her eyes and was terrified and confused and ran to the exit door on the roof and fled the building. I told her that was not her brother but the devil tempting her to kill herself and possibly trying to destroy her soul. With much discussion among the four trainees/counselees, she became convinced that it was not her brother trying to encourage her to commit suicide, but an evil force meant to destroy her.

She was very relieved and stated that she had no more desire to go to that building again and instead she would go to church and pray for her brother's soul.

After the week of counseling/training we had a couple days to tour the country and city. I have never seen a city so full of people and was so very clean. I was told that if you spit on the sidewalk you would be arrested and until you paid a fine you would be in jail.

Wow, no wonder why the city was so clean.

We toured a beautiful Buddha temple where a female Buddha was worshipped. I was surprised that there was a female Buddha. The lady attendant showing us around said that Buddha has 1,000 faces but one is female. I said that the statue looked like the Mother of Jesus, the Blessed Virgin Mary. She agreed and said that many of the worshipers also thought of her as the Mother of Jesus. What a surprise!

My Jesus, You are omni present.

Our trip to Singapore was full of all kinds of surprises. Tall, beautiful buildings, dozens and dozens of high-rise apartment buildings, beautifully designed and well kept. Even more beautiful were the business buildings in the downtown area. One group of very classy design of a group of 5 buildings consisted of 5 tall edifices shaped like a hand with 4 of them in a semicircle and the 5th in the middle. The locals called the fifth finger the "thumb." Not a scrap of paper on the streets and older people, men and women sweeping the streets 24 hours every day. Inside the buildings spotless chrome and shiny brass and spotless clean glass everywhere. Neatly uniformed guides willing to answer questions and guide us to our destination. Overall, a very beautiful Chinese country.

Chapter 25

France

Our trip to Strasberg France was another 80-hour training and counseling week. No one stood out in my group but the day before we started the sessions. I noticed that one of the attending counselor group ladies was acting very jittery, and nervous. She looked exhausted and sad. I asked her if she was alright, to which she answered,

"No, I don't think I should be here."

I told her to come with us (Luci and I) and we would find a comfortable place to sit and talk. As we began to talk, the woman revealed that she had volunteered to come to this meeting so that she could counsel others who had an abortion. After we had found a quiet and private place, the woman began to weep and said that she had had an abortion as a young girl twenty years ago and that she was haunted by that decision, unable to live in peace with the memory or with herself. In my experience, this was a typical reaction of a mother who had aborted her child, but she was not yet healed. She should have not been there as a counselor.

After hearing her out, I reassured her that the week was not only to learn the counseling technique of Hope Alive counseling, but that it would be an opportunity for her to talk about her abortion and begin the process of healing.

"I was afraid to tell my story because I thought you'd send me away," The woman said.

Once again, I reassured her that that would not happen. She agreed to stay and see what happened during the week. She was not in my group and I'm sure she got a lot of help in another group. On the last day before we broke up and went our own way, she came up to us and thanked Luci and I for encouraging her to say. She had a good but hard week and she looked somewhat relieved. I did not know whose group she was in and didn't ask to keep the confidentiality intact. Still, I pray for her at times and ask God to protect her and to continue healing her.

After accomplishing this massive training/counseling schedule again we were now more than fully trained and experienced and did our counseling here in Hawaii with 4 clients at a time for the next 10 years. Both of us Luci and I provided the counseling free of charge, which usually lasted around 32 sessions, once or twice a week, with each session lasting three hours or more. The results were dramatic and lifesaving. Those who we counseled were healed, forgiven, knew the names and the gender of their lost children, accepted them into their families and had tools to cope with whatever came along in their life journey and had themselves returned to God. We continued the counseling program for those beautiful and rewarding 10 years until Luci was no longer able to participate due to her declining health.

We were blessed with the help of Sister Geralyn Spaulding OSB from the Benedictine Monastery. During her first session assisting us, she told me about a vision that she had: She said,

"I saw Jesus standing next to you when you were giving the introductory remarks. He looked right at me and said, "This is what want you to do." I know for sure that from this revelation He wants me to help you your work," she told me later.

Chapter 26

Our Turn

Luci and I prepared for and held an international Hope Alive meeting (IHACA) in Hawaii in 1992, with ten countries in attendance. Overall, it was a successful conference academically and including a day tour to many beautiful Hawaiian sites. Dr Ney ran the whole weeks agenda with teaching and storytelling, similar to, but not as dramatic as the ones that we experienced in the European and Asian countries since these were already trained counselors.

A few months later, Luci and I organized and conducted a training here in Hawaii for all who were interested. We had two women from Australia. One of the ladies from Australia, who was originally from Peru, admitted that she had been raped and was forced to married the man. He was an ogre and dictator who abused her and kept raping her until she had birthed four children over the course of the long and torturous years. He was a high-ranking executive in a Australian Oil Company. Every day before He went to work, he locked the refrigerator so that his wife couldn't get food to feed the children. He was an abusive dictator and was simply not a nice man or husband. he had passed away at a young age and she felt free now to live a happy and peaceful life and raise her children as best she could.

It was here that we were introduced to Pat, who later helped us get to the proper surgeon in Oxnard, California for Luci's surgery on both of her internal carotid arteries. We also met a lady from Oahu, Hawaii, who was a pencil drawing artist and a deacon and his wife from Maui. No one from our group of counselees had had an abortion, but had suffered neglect, abandonment and sexual and physical abuse.

Looking back at it, the week went exceptionally well. The lady who was an artist had a tremendous talent for pencil drawings. She had brought many pencil drawings with her of a beautiful woman with very sad eyes, and I suspected that she was drawing herself because she was also very good looking despite those sad eyes. From what I could tell, her art was gallery-ready, and she wanted to sell copies of her paintings but did not have the money to have the copies made. One evening when most trainees were in their rooms doing their Hope Alive homework, Luci and I went to her room and gave he a check for $2,000.00 seed money to get prints made for sale. She was so shocked and grateful and stated that she had prayed for help from God and that we were an answer to her prayers.

Thank you, God, for giving us the means to help her.

One evening at home in Hawaii, my mother called me to let us know that her sister Edith's husband, my Uncle Eddie Wanous, had passed away. As soon as I hung up the phone, I had a vision of Uncle Eddie being led by two angels skyward to Heaven. I called my mother back and told her of my vision and she was immediately at peace and would pass that on to her sister.

While in Hawaii, I started a monthly men's Christian Lunch program at the Large Pearl Harbor Enlisted Men's Club. With the proper promotion, we had a great turn-out. I invited Pastors (one at a time) from all different Christian denominations to come and speak. The topic that I insisted upon was always their testimony and how they found God in their life. A few months later, the club manager gave us an upgrade room because he was impressed by what we were doing. He ended up attending the monthly Christian Testimony sessions.

O God, You, are so wonderful and generous.

Through this connection, the 1ˢᵗ Assembly of God pastor who I had come and spoken with more than once, invited me to preach twice at his Waikiki Beach Ministry in front of the Sheraton Hotel on the beach in the early morning. I later also started a Businessman's Christian Lunch held at St. Andrews Episcopal Cathedral once a week. The Episcopal Bishop was impressed and said "yes" immediately and gave us access to a lavish room which had a large conference table that held 18-20 places to sit. The format was a Lectionary gospel reading for the coming Sunday followed by discussion concerning how the reading had meaning for our lives. I also included 10 minutes meditation at the end of our meeting. It was wonderful being together and praying together by men of all faiths.

During some time of the four years that we spent in Hawaii, Luci got a call from her younger sister Geraldine (Gerry) who told her that she was having big problems with her Real Estate Company in San Louis Obispo California. Her problem was overstaffing with too many agents, and accountant and a lawyer. Gerry really wasn't a people manager. She asked Luci to come and help her clean house and rid of her associates and employees so she could work independently again. I agreed to let Luci go.

We had allowed Gerry to live with us for a year when we were stationed in Bethesda, Maryland at the Naval Dental School. I relented to let Luci go, thinking she would be gone a few weeks or a month at the most. I knew that I would be lonely, especially on weekends when I wasn't working. After she was gone, I started to go out to the Benedictine Monastery on Friday night after work and staying until after Sunday night prayers (Compline) at about 8:30 PM.

While at the Monastery I also started a garden, planted 4 trees which were seedlings from pine trees near St. James Church in Medjugoria, worked with Father Michael tending and extracting honey from the bee colony, made wax candles for the tabernacle light, re-roofed the main house with Father Michael, did major trimming of trees near the main house, helped dig out soil by hand from the north side of the house which eventually made room for Fr, David and Fr. Michael to build a lower level creating space to build two bedrooms, two baths and a space for 3 washers and 3 dryers.

I ate meals with the community, attended daily Mass and joined in the daily prayers 3 times a day, in addition I slept on the floor in the Chapel with a pillow and blanket at the end of the day when the Grand Silence began. Before Christmas I made 6 wooden plaques with a copy of Our

Lady of Vladimir photo glued on the front surface and then covered with layers of varnish to preserve and seal the images. For Christmas, I gave each of our children one copy and one to my mother and kept one for one for us.

Luci was gone 6 months and I think her sister wanted and tried to convince Luci to leave me and stay and get into real estate with her. Still, despite everything, Luci came home. I gained tremendous learning and habits during that 6-month period. My prayer life was deeply enriched, especially the rosary. My attendance at Mass became more focused and attentive and my respect for those who gave their lives, both men and women to the religious and clergy life in a monastery grew considerably. In addition, I saw that the commitment to religious life in community was not easy. It was like any family of individuals, there were many conflicts. So is life.

Looking back at it, I can say with confidence that it was one of the best six months that I ever experienced being there, working and praying with the Benedictine community.

Chapter 27

Maryland

In 1980, I was transferred to the Navy Graduate Dental School in Bethesda, Maryland, and was assigned as the Assistant Dean of Students. It was a multitasking type of job, but I did alright. I did, however, really miss the patients and clinical dentistry. I would sneak down to the clinic one or two times a week to keep my skills up and to do the things I loved the most, treating patients. I also joined the Gold Foil Club and did a lot of gold foils in the evening on students, wives of students, and among other faculty members who requested gold foils. There was never a shortage of patients available.

While still in Bethesda, I started hearing rifle gunshots in my head. These noises were always single shots, that occurred frequently enough to be a concern. I know what a rifle gunshot sounds like since I had been a hunter all my life. This lasted only a few weeks, but they got my attention. I told my civilian neighbor, Frank McLaughlin, about what I was experiencing, and he said I was just overworked. I didn't believe that theory. After organizing, leading, and completing an in-house, week-long, Navy continuing education course, I went over to the Psychology department of the Navy Hospital in Bethesda and told them about the gun shots and they said I had "Combat Fatigue" called PTSD now a days and admitted me to the psych ward.

I wasn't too happy about that and in fact, I was embarrassed. I spent the first week extremely tense and unsure of my sanity. I was so tense that a very kind nurse came every night and massaged my back just so I could go to sleep. She did this on her own without me requesting it.

Did the Holy Spirit send her?

The second week I spent caring for the other patients; often encouraging others either one-on-one or in group counseling, who were struggling with a variety of problems. On one occasion, I slipped a Miraculous medal of the Blessed Mother into a lady's hand who was in a straitjacket. She smiled at me.

Mother Mary, please take care of her.

Later when driving across country to my final duty station in Idaho Falls, Idaho, I stopped to see a deer hunting buddy of mine, Gary Moore, in Montana only to find out he had committed suicide. He had gone up into the mountains and shot himself. His partner had stolen his retirement money that he had saved, to invest in a semi-truck and trailer business and I guess that was too much for him to handle. The date of his death coincided with the days that I had heard the gunshots. That answered many questions for me. I pray for him daily now, his wife and seven children (3 sets of twins and one single birth), and all people who have died of suicide that Jesus would forgive them and bring them to Eternal joy in His kingdom.

Chapter 28

Idaho

My final duty station was at the Branch Dental Clinic, Idaho Falls, Idaho. The Navy ordered built a beautiful Dental Clinic utilizing a double-wide trailer. It had 3 operatories, one for dental officer patient care and one for Hygiene. Another small space for storage for cleaning gear. It had a a front desk to greet patients and space for record storage and another space for an office for me, the director of the clinic. However, they forgot an important element during the construction, the clinic had no weather insulation as well as no heat source during the first winter when the wind chill factor lowered to -70 degrees below zero. Under these bitter cold circumstances, we were rendered completely unable to work. We sat around for a while in our heavy coats and gloves and had to close the clinic for a few days until the weather warmed up. When the next Spring arrived the Navy hired an insulation crew and added a gas heater, and we were happy for that when Winter came again.

Admiral Buckley

About once a quarter Admiral John D. Buckley, U.S. Navy, (nicknamed 'The Sea Wolf') came to Idaho Falls to talk to the prospective Commanders of Nuclear Navy Aircraft Carriers, Cruisers, and Submarines. I think he must have looked up my records because he always stopped in alone at my Dental Clinic, which was situated just outside the local airport, and wanted to talk story about the experience that I had on the battleship USS New Jersey, BB62. He also talked a lot about his experiences during WWII, Korea, and later. He told me he retired with the rank of Captain and was later called back to active-duty and became the Ship and Fleet Inspector General. His WWII experience was as Commander of PT Boat Squadron-3 of which he commanded one and five other PT boats under his Command, including Lt. John F. Kennedy who skippered PT-109 also in the Pacific.

Later, President Kennedy promoted Captain Buckley to Rear Admiral. The Admiral received the Medal of Honor for bravery and heroics in the many Pacific conflicts that he encountered. Buckley was personally involved in sinking enemy submarines, war ships as well as enemy merchant ships. He was one of the most decorated officers of the Second World War. He was in the Normandy Invasion, clearing the way for personnel landing crafts. He also picked up many survivors from the ocean, including enemy survivors.

After the War, and while still on active duty, he turned his attention to a new phase of his career as he was assigned as the Director of New ship inspections. He told me that when he would approach a ship about to be inspected, he would wear wrinkled and dirty coveralls, a very old and salty hat with scrambled eggs on the brow, and one single dirty looking ribbon attached to his coveralls haphazardly, the Medal of Honor. Upon approaching the Quarter Deck rendering a rather sloppy salute and requesting permission to come aboard, the officer of the deck would wonder who this character was and would ask him for his identification papers. Admiral Buckley would simply say,

"Tell your Captain that Admiral Buckley is on the Quarter Deck and is ready to begin the ship's Inspection."

Well, as you can imagine, all hell broke loose, and the Captain and XO came running immediately to the Quarter Deck to escort the Admiral to the Captain's stateroom. Admiral Buckley really enjoyed the surprise tactic and his main purpose in the surprise announcement of his presence, however, was to see how good the ship's security was and how fast they could react. Another example of this tactic was when Admiral Buckley was the Commanding Officer of the Clarksville Base in Tennessee and not losing any of his wartime daring and fun, he would change himself by donning a ninja suit and with a blackened face, and attempt to penetrate a security location on Base. It kept the security folks on their toes. Again, good security, but crazy methods. He was a real character. I loved that man.

After his retirement, the navy named a new guided missile destroyer the USS Buckley DDG-64 after the Admiral. He retired with 55 years of service in the United States Navy. He died at the age of 84 and is buried at Arlington Cemetery. I'll never forget him and his fun-loving ways. He was a good friend. I miss him.

I was able to counsel the enlisted members of my staff In Idaho Falls who had many emotional problems as well as the young Lieutenant just out of Dental School. I started a ministry at the local jail which focused on the Gospel readings for the coming Sunday. We had 3-5 participants and I had two female volunteers to help assist. I found the biggest drama was with the ladies from church who came to assist me. One of them wanted to give her phone number to one of the inmates so she could "continue to support him after he got out of jail." This was very misdirected and dangerous. I spent as much time counseling my support staff as those who were incarcerated. Our ministry there did not last long. I had my first Spiritual Director while in Idaho Falls. He was gay and was doing his best to live a celibate life. We ended up counseling each other.

One of my new friends was a Nuclear Engineer at the site in the Arco desert. His name is lost in my memory. We did a lot of long distance running together as well as skiing the slopes on the Idaho side of the Grand Teton Mountain range. The function of the site was to utilize the 3 nuclear reactor prototypes for upkeep and training. The prototypes were installed in a mock Submarine, Aircraft carrier, and Cruiser. Another friend Chuck Solbrig, also a nuclear engineer, worked at the site in the Arco Desert and was also a deacon at the Holy Family Catholic Church in Idaho Falls. I was able to ask him a lot of questions about the Deaconate Formation Program and his thoughts and feelings about his time so far as being a Deacon. He also had a depression problem and I befriended him so that I could help him emotionally. He and his wife, Carol, finally got couples counseling and that helped a lot. I think his basic problem was that he felt unloved. I noticed that every time he and Carol were with us after their bout with counseling she would say "I love you" to Chuck often and he would smile. I was trying to discern if I should go to Deaconate formation and eventually applied In Idaho but was turned down because I didn't have enough time left at that duty station and I was about to retire from the Navy. I retired from the Navy one year later in 1985.

Chapter 29

Hawaii Again

After retirement from the Navy, Luci and I went back to Hawaii to live the rest of our lives. I started working as a civilian dentist with Dr. Craig Mason, a dentist who had previously worked for me at Pearl Harbor when we were stationed there in the Navy as a Lieutenant. Luci worked for me as my dental assistant for a few months until I had made enough money to hire someone else to assist me.

While Luci was still assisting me, one day I had a patient who needed a porcelain crown and when I chose the color and shade of the crown, Luci disagreed with my selection. After discussing our differences, the local patient looked up at us and remarked, "Eh, are you two married?"

That was hilarious. I couldn't stop laughing.

Luci eventually went back to school to work on a Master's degree in Public Health Nursing. She eventually received a second master's degree as a Maternal Child Health and Nurse Practitioner. I also started monitoring the deacon classes being offered to deacon candidates at St Stevens Diocesan Center (previously St. Stevens Seminary) and eventually applied but was turned down because we had to leave Hawaii to take care of our parents.

Luci's mother was in and out of the hospital because of her diabetes, while my father had early Alzheimer's disease. This was my second failed attempt to enter the Diaconate formation since we decided it was more important that we go back to Minnesota to take care of our elderly parents. We felt called by God to return to Minnesota to take care of Luci's mother, Theresa and my father, Edwin. I was an only child and Luci was the oldest of 8 children, so it seemed the right and logical thing to do. We knew God would want us to go and that He would reward us somehow for our decision to give up our jobs, friends and move back to Minnesota to care for our parents.

Honor your Father and Mother

While we were there, on the first Sunday we attended mass at Immaculate Conception, our old parish, I talked to the Deacon about my two previous attempts to enter the Diaconate formation program. He told me he would call the Deacon Formation Director on Monday in St. Paul.

The next day, the director, Deacon Peter Haley called me and arranged an interview for Luci and me that same week. I applied for the 3-year Diaconate Formation program held at the St. Paul Seminary in St. Paul Minnesota. Applications were closed before I applied *(third strike and I'm out?)* but because of my extensive work in the church, counseling, and jail ministry over the years I was accepted immediately and started the formation in September 1996.

I also was told that they normally took 12 candidates but could not find the 12th one who was qualified until I applied.

Providential. Thank you, Lord.

As Luci would often say again,

"God is in charge"

I soon found myself in the role of leader of our class. I wrote a class prayer and motto. In meetings prior to the start of the formation classes, all the men were concerned that we were "not worthy" to be ordained as clergy of the Church. We were sinners! My response to them was "no one is worthy to serve the Church, everyone sins, but this is a **call** to serve, and we should be **obedient**." The question was settled, then.

Some of the candidates were there because of their spouse's influence but they were good candidates. I could tell they were good men, and their wives were good supporters. The wives were obligated to attend all classes with their husbands but not required to write all the papers assigned and did not have to preach when we took course in Homiletics. One candidate was gay but a celibate man. I was ordained as Deacon on September 30, 1999, along with my 11 other classmates, at the St. Paul Cathedral in Saint Paul, Minnesota by the Most Reverend, Arch-Bishop Patrick Flynn. My parents, Sharon and Luci's parents and a few friends attended the ordination. It was a day filled with joy and thanksgiving. It was unusual for all 12 candidates to survive the three year formation, but our class did.

In the first few months of the formation, I wondered if this was really for me until I learned that "Deaconia" translated from Greek to "servant." I then knew that I was in the right place at the right time. I completely enjoyed the classes especially the New and Old Testament. Luci and I took a wonderful two-week trip to the Holy Land (not Ireland ha ha) and were able to explore the sights where Jesus lived, traveled and preached in and was crucified in.

We had a group bus guide, which was led by a wonderful and very knowledgeable Jewish man who insisted that he was secular and not a believer. I brought a book along which was a tour guide for the places we visited as well as things that Jesus said when in those locations and beautiful prayers to accompany our journey at each location. I bought Luci a beautiful gold Jerusalem cross and chain after our boat voyage across the Sea of Jordan. She still wears it to this day.

Chapter 30

Faribault

After this trip to Israel, I purchased a 100+ year old home in Faribault, which was already an assisted care facility, from my cousin Scott Nelson and his wife Linda which was aptly called "The Inn Town House."

Luci, with another Hawaii nurse friend, Malia Kelso, an RN, MS in nursing from Hawaii, both ran it while we were in Minnesota for 6 years. Malia had to leave her job in Hawaii as an instructor for EMT ambulance drivers and care givers. I gave Malia 50% ownership in the home, because of her commitment to us, including a 1-bedroom apartment on the premises above the double garage. When Luci and Malia took over the home, most of the residents had health issues such as high blood pressure, constipation and were generally not feeling well.

After Luci and Malia started cooking fresh food with lots of vegetables, small amounts of lean meat and fruit, all the residents eventually gained their health back. Since most of the ladies in residence were Catholic, I arranged to have a Eucharistic Minister come every Sunday to distribute communion. A resident named Martha, did not talk at first, and we were told by some of the residents that she had been that way for years. We were also told it was because she had been abused for years previously by her husband. After six months of TLC from Luci and Malia, she started talking again.

Ten months later, she moved out and got her own apartment and eventually was hired by Luci and Malia to work at the Inn Town House, doing cleaning and other odd jobs like some of the cooking, serving and cleaning up around the Home. It was a total turn around for her and a blessing for us. Another lady had a picture in her room of her four sisters, who were all Dominican nuns in full habit. She was the only one of the girls in her family who did not become a religious sister. She made quilts all winter long and during the summer, spent several hours a day in the large garden in the back of the home harvesting raspberries, corn, snap peas, onions, squash and pumpkins. She also did all the weeding and made sure to keep her garden free of all weeds throughout summer. She gave Luci a beautiful hand-made quilt that took her six months to finish.

One morning, Malia called us at home early to tell us that one of the residents had passed away during the night. I told her not to do anything until we got there. Upon entering her bedroom, we noticed that she was laying on her back, with a beautiful smile on her face and her rosary beads in the hand which indicated she died while saying her rosary. As a Deacon, I said prayers for the dead and we contacted her family and the funeral home and her priest at the Catholic church at Sacred Heart. It would be a great gift if we could all pass that way, at peace and speaking the prayers of the rosary.

When Luci and I eventually went back to Hawaii, we sold our half of the home to Malia, who happily obliged with our plans.

Chapter 31

Minnesota

I had previously called a dentist friend, Ted Erickson, before we had moved back to Minnesota, and had lined up a position in his clinic called Southern Heights Dental Center. I had kept my Dental license active all those years after I graduated. I was supposed to report to work at the end of June but because the dentist whom I was to replace, Dr. Steve Springmeyer, was having severe emotional problems, they asked me to come right away. I agreed to the proposition and started working as a dentist in my hometown of Faribault on the 10th of June. I knew a lot of people because of my father's grocery business and because I went to Grade School and High School in Faribault. An interesting fact of coincidence was that Carroll Shaft, my old flame from High School had divorced and remarried Dr. Steve Springmeyer, the man I was to replace.

Ted was an innovator and a visionary and within a year we started talking about building a dental Clinic in Rochester, Minnesota, the home of the Mayo Clinic. At that time there were only "father and son/daughter" dental offices in Rochester. We saw the opening and with financial assistance from the local Dental Insurance Company HDS, we bought the land and built a 10,000-square-foot dental clinic right next door to the sprawling IBM complex of buildings, which was where most of our patients eventually came from. I helped interview dentists to hire and we were open for business ahead of construction schedule completion and under budget. Many of our early patients were welfare but it was a start. We eventually added an orthodontist, a periodontist, and an oral surgeon. I worked pro bono two days a week, for two years while Dr Poppenburg worked one day for over a year. We both commuted from Faribault.

The third dentist who I had interviewed and hired worked five days each week, including Saturday. I stayed in a Day's Inn one night to complete my two-day stay. We were able to pay off our debt in three years and hire three more general dentists to complete our staff. After four years had passed, we sold shares and partnerships to four, highly skilled dentists for $ 250,000 each. We slowly backed out of the business with significant monthly checks until their purchase of the practice was complete.

During my practice in Faribault, there were a lot of Mexican migrants who immigrated to Faribault and at first, they were on welfare which paid about half of our usual customary fees. I was the only one to take them as patients, but in the end, I observed how Mexican couples both became employed and had dual insurance so they could afford crowns and bridges and any dental work needed without a co-pay. God awarded me for taking these good people who worked hard to have a better life in good USA. During this time, I was ordained as a deacon and was helping take care of my father. We eventually went back to Hawaii after 6 years in Minnesota and brought my Mom and Dad with us.

Ted finally retired at the age of seventy and he and his wife Jamie built a town house in the Minneapolis-St. Paul area. He sold his farm and home to one of his Dentist partners for a song and moved to Minneapolis after his town house was built. Ted passed away in his sleep at the age of seventy-one in his new home. His death was very unexpected, and a sad occasion for all of us.

A special story

When I was a small boy, aged around seven years old, my mother and I lived with my Grandma Ragna Nelson in Faribault for a year in 1945-46 while my dad served in Germany in the US Army. Her large home was located next to a Congregational Church. One day I wandered to the front door of the church and found it to be open. I went in and looked around. I found a small collection box with some money in it next to the front door. As I recall it was only a few coins and probably less than a dollar. I took it. Bad boy!

Some forty years later, when we moved back to Minnesota to take care of our parents, I was driving past this same Congregational Church, and I remembered what I had done. The next day I wrote a cheque for $100.00 to the Church and went to the rectory where the minister lived. I told him the story of how I had taken the money out of the poor box as a child and presented the cheque to him. To make a long story short, after a long discussion, I became his spiritual director and close friend.

The church had a small chapel in the back with six large stained-glass windows all made by Tiffany. I remember the vivid colors and the artistry of their construction. I don't think many people in Faribault know of the treasures hidden in the chapel of the Congregational Church. Later I had another Spiritual director, an African American Episcopal priest who was assigned as chaplain to the Shattuck Military Academy in Faribault. He kept falling asleep during our sessions and I quit that counseling after a few sessions. We became friends anyway and we did a few marriages together, especially mixed Catholic and Episcopal couples. We are still good friends and communicate two or three times a year.

I had another spiritual director in Faribault who was a young priest and a pastor of Sacred Heart church, which was his first assignment after his seminary studies and ordination. We were talking one evening and because of some words I said to him, he began to cry. We reversed roles and I became his spiritual director. We had a wonderful and gentle relationship, and I am sure he is still a happy man.

"I will send people to you."

A couple of years later, he was assigned to the Saint Paul Seminary to be a spiritual director for the novice priest candidates. I'm sure he did well. He was a truly wonderful man.

I also made friends with an Episcopal priest, Fr. Henry Doyle, who was the chaplain at Shaddock Military Academy in Faribault. He did many summer marriages of former students from Shaddock and St. Mary's, a private girl's school, and when the couple was mixed

Catholic/Protestant he would invite me to con-celebrate the wedding with him, which took place in Episcopal, Methodist, Lutheran, and Evangelical Churches. I found this to be quite fun and interesting.

I started a prison ministry at the State Prison in Faribault every Tuesday evening. This lasted three and a half years when we moved back to Hawaii. During our two-hour sessions, we discussed the next Sunday Gospel reading and how it would apply to us. One of the participants was the Mexican gang leader in the prison. He brought three Compadres with him to each session. He was eventually baptized, confirmed, and received the Eucharist all the same day, Easter Sunday morning in the Prison library. His life was transformed. He, did, however, remain as the Mexican Gang leader. His message to his gang members was new and changed from violence to,

"You have an opportunity to become a better person in prison. Get an education or trade. Work on that and I will protect you."

There were other dramatic experiences of conversion and change of attitude for the better during those prison ministry days. Since I had bad experiences with untrained volunteers in the past, I decided to do the work alone and it worked out fine.

Chapter 32

My Parents

Before I was ordained, my parents were about to celebrate their 60th wedding anniversary. Our Pastor, Father Kevin Finnigan, agreed to have a special Anniversary Mass for them during one of the regularly scheduled Mass times. He said to me,

"Why don't you preach?"

I immediately said "NO! because the idea of preaching scared me.

After thinking about it, however, I said "Yes."

I was afraid because I had not yet taken the homiletics course in my formation. I looked up some homilies about anniversaries and weddings and they all looked dull and "boilerplate" to me. I decided to ask my mother what their secret was to survive 60 years of marriage. Her answer was immediate, "We never go to bed without forgiving each other!" I realized then that is what God did for all of us: He forgave us our weaknesses, sins, and failures daily and my mother and dad were doing the same, following God's example. Forgiveness became the theme of my homily and it went well and I felt very comfortable. I was ordained on September 30, 1999, at the St. Paul Cathedral and began ministering as a deacon in the three combined Catholic churches in Faribault, along with three priests. The Europeans who immigrated to that area in the 1800's and later, founded the three churches, French (Sacred Heart church), Irish (Immaculate Conception church), and German (St Lawrence church). Eventually, the three churches were united at a new location, in the middle of corn fields just south of town, and a new church called "Divine Mercy' was born. I was never fortunate enough to minister in that new church.

***

We purchased a home near my parents in Faribault on Roberd's Lake but eventually, they had to move in with us. We all shared in the caring of my father.

Chapter 33

Immaculate Conception Church

My first mass at Immaculate Conception church to assist and preach was an exciting and scary experience for me despite feeling well prepared to preach. I guess my fear was partly because this was my hometown and most of the people already knew me and my family. A reception for me, Luci and my family was to follow the mass in the grade school hall. I came late to the reception because so many well-wishers held me captive in the Sacristy congratulating me and offering many kind words.

As soon as I entered the reception hall my mother asked me to take my father (who was in a wheelchair by now) to the bathroom. We struggled to get there, because it wasn't in the same building, and I eventually got my dad sitting on the toilet. He had a bowel movement after much grunting. I tore off some toilet paper and handed it to him. He looked at me puzzled and did not know what to do with it, so I had to, for the first time, wipe him clean. As I was doing this, the words came into my heart from God,

"Do not be proud, this is what I want you to do. Humble yourself."

By the time I got my dad back to the hall, the reception was over, and I realized that God didn't want me to be proud of my new status as a deacon, but He wanted me to get down, be humble and serve, if necessary, with all my efforts to help His children, His people, and specifically my family. My "caregiving ministry" lasted thirty-two years and involved my father Eddie, my mother Marie, and my wife Lucille. Luci has now been in a foster care home since April 22, 2019.

After helping my mother taking care of my father for about 11 years, I soon realized that my mother would need help in her older life. I also knew that Luci was not far behind.

The Mexicans in Faribault

Interestingly, after some observation of the Mexican immigration to Faribault, due to the many job openings in the variety of factories in town and the area, I eventually realized most of them were born and raised Catholic in Mexico. They were Catholics for nearly 5 centuries due to the appearance of the Blessed Mother Mary to a humble Inca peasant, recently converted to the Catholic church named Juan Diego on Tepeyac hill near Mexico City. Eventually a cathedral was built in memory of "Our Lady of Guadalupe on that site. The Catholic church in Faribault and the surrounding communities was not experiencing a significant influx of immigrant numbers. There were only a few immigrants at our Sunday masses at Sacred Heart church where the only Spanish language mass was celebrated. I discovered that two different Evangelical churches were displaying an image of our Lady of Guadalupe in their sanctuary and going to meet the new

Mexican arrivals in their homes and inviting them to their church, often speaking to them in Spanish. I could stand on the front steps of Sacred Heart Church and see both Evangelical churches in view at the same time. I made a plan.

My son Michael had sent me a life-size copy of the original image of Our Lady of Guadalupe from Mexico City. A friend made a frame for it and I made two large signs made which were posted above the front and side doors of the Sacred Heart Church which read "Benvenuto" (Welcome.) I then planned a large special mass in Spanish to celebrate the Enthronement of the Image of our Lady of Guadalupe to be in an alcove to the right of the altar and tabernacle with votive candles and a prayer kneeler at its foot.

Our lady was facing the altar where her Son, through the priest, provided the miracle of the consecration (transubstantiation) of the bread and wine into His Holy body and blood at every mass. On the day of the Enthronement Mass, I invited and had one bishop as the main celebrant, three priests assisting, and myself as Deacon. The church was full. The Mexican people showed up in local and Native Inca costumes with children and adults dancing down the aisle in a great and joyful procession. With lots of bells, dancing, prayers, and incense our Lady was properly enthroned to the joy of all. Typically, our Spanish mass had approximately 50 in attendance before the enthronement and after the enthronement, the attendance grew to 250 and kept growing. The priests of our 3 churches were sent to Mexico one at a time to be immersed in the Spanish language for one month each. A Mexican lady was given a paid position on the church staff who acted as the liaison and problem solver for the Mexican community.

All praise to God!

Another Priest who was an associate of the pastor of our church was struggling with some problems because every time I saw him, he didn't look happy. One day when he was alone in his office I knocked and asked him If I could come in and talk for a while. It turned out that his father wanted him to follow him into his Insurance Company business in Chicago and was very disappointed when his son became a priest. The father's negative reaction to his son's decision to enter the seminary followed him for many years and acted like a weight on his shoulders during his formation and after his ordination. He felt abandoned by his father and was not able to cope with the coldness his father expressed toward him. During our conversation, he opened up to me and began to cry and his pain was obvious. I suggested that he take a sabbatical and spend the time away to decide whether to please his father or to please God. With prayer and advice from friends, he applied to study Cannon Law at Catholic University in Washington D.C. He was a successful student and after graduation he was assigned as a Cannon lawyer in the Arch Diocese of St. Paul. He was now a lawyer and a priest. He and his father have reconciled, and both are happy and reunited again as a loving father and son.

"I will send people to you."

Chapter 34

Oblate Retreat

After ordination, I started a men's prayer group in my home. Knowing that I would be going back to Hawaii eventually, I wanted this group to last, because so many things that I had started didn't continue after I left, so I decided to take the men to St. John's Abbey in St. Cloud Minnesota to an Oblate retreat. After the retreat, I invited the Director of Oblates, Fr. John Brennen OSB to join us in Faribault for two of our men's monthly meetings. He was a down-to-earth farm boy from Minnesota and was one of twelve children. He taught us a few new curse words from his farm days with his six brothers. The mildest one was "Holy Shit." I guess he thought that was a religious saying that passed the test. He was funny and fun and just the type of hang-loose priest the guys needed.

At the following annual Oblate retreat, the men made their Oblation to become Oblates of the Benedictine Order. They are still meeting twenty-four years later every Saturday morning at the Robert's Lake resort pavilion, to share breakfast, pray, and catch up on their struggles and joys of life. Some of them still go to St. Johns Abbey for the annual Oblate retreat which has excellent speakers, usually priests or brothers from the abbey. There are about 100 monks in residence at this time. One of our members who became an Oblate was Billy, who had spent fifty years at the Faribault School for the mentally challenged, previously called "The Dink School" by us very immature high school students. He came with us on every trip to the Abbey and met with us every time without fail on Saturday mornings. He was released from the school due to a change in the level of mental problems exhibited and routinely tested for the with the other residents and because my father had sponsored him and given him a job delivering the St. Paul Pioneer Express and dispatch and a place to live. Thanks Dad.

At one point, as I had mentioned previously, I had sold enough "starts" to earn enough points to get a 22-caliber rifle, the first gun I ever owned. I spent many Saturdays down by the Straight River. One day while hunting, I started thinking about Billy. I realized that I had not seen him for a few weeks, and he missed a meeting on Saturday morning. After giving him many rides home, I knew where Billy lived. I went to the house where my dad rented Billy a room and found Billy in bed and I couldn't wake him. His pants were full of feces, and I called an ambulance, and they took him to the hospital. He was dehydrated and delirious and after lots of IV fluids and some food, he recovered and lived many years after that. When I'm in Minnesota, which isn't often, I join them at their Saturday meetings. I remind the other members of our group that when we would go to St. Johns Abbey for the annual Oblate Retreat, we were always still in the workaholic world and walking fast to and from buildings but Billy couldn't keep up with our pace so we had to slow down, and walk at Billy's pace.

This turned out to be a gift, which we all recognized knowing that we not only had learned to slow our walking but to also slow our minds and to start focusing on Jesus and the retreat.

Chapter 35

Returning to Hawaii

My father's Alzheimer's disease advanced rapidly and after 6 years of severe winters, we decided to go back to Hawaii and take my parents with us. Luci's mother had passed away due to a car accident. My father passed away one month after we returned to Hawaii. We sent his body back to Kohl's funeral home and he was interred in a cemetery in Blooming Prairie, Minnesota. I settled my mother in a condo in Harbor Court where we lived in Hawaii, and we were able to see her every day. She lived another eleven years and passed away at the age of ninety-one. She was in and out of hospitals and re-hab facilities which continued for those 11 years. She and my father are now buried together in the cemetery in Blooming Prairie, Minnesota, my mother's original home. My mother's parents and grandparents are also interred there, as well as a couple of her aunts and uncles.

While still in Minnesota, Luci received a significant inheritance from her namesake Aunt Lucille Jewett We talked about what to do with the money, to save it, or to travel and see the world. So, guess what option we chose? We took cruises and land travel and saw the world.

On one early trip, we spent twenty-one days in Ireland and had no hotel reservations, just a rental car. We found B&B's and other places similar along the way for the night. We went first to Achill Island, in County Mayo to the "Our Lady Queen of Peace House of Prayer" where we visited with Katherine Gallagher, who was a mystic and had the five Passion Wounds of Christ during Passion Week as well as bruises on her shoulders from the heavy cross. Katherine's main gift was to counsel men and women religious and clergy. Father Gerard McInney was her spiritual director and who was present during most weekends at that time and to celebrate mass. We knew of them because they had both visited the Benedictine Monastery of Hawaii where she had given spiritual talks to a few groups and individual counseling for those that had gathered at the monastery. After mass at the prayer center in Achill Island, we purchased a few things from the gifts store such as holy medals, prayer cards, and books. We had a nice long Chat with Katherine before we left, and she said a prayer over Luci and me. Father McInney took us to St. Patrick's College in Maynooth, Northern Ireland where he was the Dean of the college. We stayed for 2 days and had private Mass both days with Father McGinnity who celebrated the mass. After we departed the College, we stayed in a small Cistercian Monastery which he recommended close by for the first night out. It reminded me so much of Thomas Merton.

We found a variety of lodging along the way and met some wonderful innkeepers. We also stayed one night in an old castle which was partially renovated into guest rooms. I had to learn to drive on the left side of the road real fast especially motoring along lanes with very tall stone boundary fences that gave us no lateral vision to see who was coming around the bend of the road and some were coming fast, not to mention the geese, sheep, goats and cows who thought they owned the road. I guess they did! Every few miles there were roundabouts where everyone seemed to drive faster when on them.

We visited many Castles and ruins of castles where the only thing remaining was the tower that the Irish would have hidden in within when the Vikings were pillaging their farm, village or Monastery. We did visit Blarney Castle where if you kissed the Blarney stone you would have good luck for the rest of your life. To kiss the Blarney Stone, you had to walk up three stories of a narrow crumbling stairwell two feet wide and no handrail and then lay on your back, scooch backwards about 2 feet, and then raise your head to kiss the stone. Nevertheless, Luci did not want to do the acrobatics to do that little act. The lady who brought us up to the Blarney Stone area held a camera and who I thought would take my picture kissing the stone. But she didn't. Instead, she was chewing her sandwich when I emerged.

I asked, "Why didn't you take my picture?"

She said, "Well, Laddy, I had to eat my Luunch!" (how she said it) in the most beautiful Irish brogue I have ever heard. She eventually took my photo with a Polaroid, and we went on our way. We drove around the Ring of Carry and visited County Clark where Luci's grandparents immigrated from. We stopped in a pub for lunch and a pint of Guinness and inquired about any Clarks who might be relatives and we were directed to the courthouse where all the family records were kept. It was late and by then Luci was tired, so we went on our way. We visited the Crystal Factory in Galway and made some purchases which were mailed home for us. We stayed in an old Manor house one night and they said it was haunted. Luci didn't sleep all night because she was afraid of ghosts, and I slept like a log. We stayed a few days in Dublin and toured the Guinness Factory, attended a play at the Abbey Theater, and spent a great evening in an old pub with all the Irish who loved to sing and do the jig, and of course, would never turn down a pint from a Yank. We Also visited Trinity University and saw the Book of Kells, said to be Ireland's greatest cultural treasure. Dr. John Seah, my friend from Hawaii had gone to school there.

On another trip, we took Debbie with us, to Elmshorn, Germany where Grandpa Bill immigrated from in 1895 when he was 5 years old. His parents had moved there from Denmark after Grandpa Bill was born. I was a typical small village with a wall all around it and a Lutheran church in the middle. It was cold and rainy, so we were discouraged from doing any ancestor searching so we stayed for a great German meal and left because Debbie had to get back to her Navy job.

She was stationed with the Navy in London, England. Luci and I came to visit Debbie a year later and stayed with her in her small flat in Kensington, near the royal residence of Charles and Diana. I ran the London Marathon while I was there. The start of the marathon was at two different parks a few miles away from each other and after both groups started at the same time, by a loud cannon boom.

The runners merged at the 18-kilometer mark, and you could hear them coming before we met because of all the yelling from both groups. The race ended in front of a statue of Sir Lord Nelson at the entrance to Buckingham Palace, where the Queen lived. We ate lots of fish and chips while we were there. And enjoyed a trip to Leeds which was an ancient and fortified city surrounded by water.

Chapter 36

Czechoslovakia

Our trip to Czechoslovakia was memorable. We were put in touch with friends of friends who lived in Prague and were willing to take us to the village that Grandma Anna (Dusek) where my maternal grandmother was also born in 1895, same as Grandpa Bill. We were able to meet them in Prague and we stayed with them overnight in their home and left the next day for the village Elbe, named after the river Elbe, that flowed through the village. It took about a two-hour drive to get there from Prague.

After we arrived we were given a tour of the village and found out that after WWI half of the residents, approximately 2,500, migrated to the US because one of the main industries for the women, who made a living crocheting doilies, table cloths, bed spreads, etc., was being taken over by machines and made for less money than the hand-made ones, so they couldn't sell theirs and their money source dried up.

We went to Catholic mass on Sunday where all the relatives went on Sundays and the priest gathered all of the children around him and that is how he did his homily. So well done and inspiring. He spoke only in Czech so we didn't understand a word he said, but you could see that the children were very happy. We were shown the beautiful ceramic baptismal font that we assumed Grandma Anna was baptized in. It looked ancient but well preserved. Outside in the back of the church was a small cemetery and many of the names were Grandma Anna's ancestors whose last name was Dusek and Schumann.

That night about eight people who were distant relatives came to dinner to meet us at the home we were staying in. Most of them spoke good English so we were able to communicate. After dinner, we had peppermint schnapps, a brandy kind of liquor and the party got very joyful. We left the next morning and made our way back to Prague. We toured the "City of Spires" which was the name given to Prague because everywhere you looked you could see many Church steeples. This turned out to be our best ancestor trip.

Chapter 37

Kristiansand

While on a cruise to the Scandinavian countries of Norway, Denmark, and Sweden, we took a 2-day trip to Kristiansand, Norway, the seaside city where my Nelson ancestor, my Grandfather, Obert Nelson had immigrated from. It had a beautiful bay and was mostly known to have the best Zoo in Scandinavia. Instead of visiting the Zoo, we walked around the small town, and I bought a 100-year-old Lithograph of a view of the city from a high point at the edge of the water, anticipating to give it to my father as a gift.

Lo and behold in the newspaper the next morning was a photo of the same view taken the day before and that view had not changed in 150 years as far as I could tell. I saved the picture, had it framed, and gave my father both framed prints when we got home. We also got to tour Oslo, Norway, the arena where the Nobel Prize was awarded. I bought some beautiful amber jewelry for Lucy and a large heavy Norwegian crystal bowl and candle sticks set.

Our whole tour of Scandinavia was sponsored by a medical and dental group which included a train, bus tour and including a medium-sized cruise ship down the fjords of Norway. At one stop during the fjords cruise, we took a helicopter ride to the top of a huge glacier. I bought a beautiful Norwegian wool handmade sweater for both Luci and me at a gift shop. She later washed hers in the washing machine with hot water and it shrunk to doll- size and she had to give it away to Good Will. *Poor Girl!* This trip was before the world warming trend which we are experiencing now so the glaciers were totally intact. The bus rides were often in the mountains and to avoid snow plowing and avalanches, the roads around the mountain edge were enclosed so it felt like a tunnel that went for miles. They were well-lit and felt very safe. The Norwegians were very inventive.

All the Scandinavian people, especially the men all looked like they could be my brothers or cousins or fathers or uncles. I felt the aura of being in my place of origin and it seemed very comfortable and down home to me. I was attracted to the accent when they spoke English and loved the rhythm of the Norwegian language. I also loved the food, especially the salted Cod and Halibut and pickled Herring.

I am proud that after the Vikings plundered and looted Ireland, Scotland and the English coast communities, they became a peaceful civilization staying neutral in the great wars and still are a very peaceful and beautiful race.

My heritage country

Chapter 38

Wailua

When we moved to Hawaii we lived on the North Shore in Waialua and my first Deacon assignment was St. Michael's Church. We also had a mission church named Saints Peter and Paul at Waimea Bay the big surf tournament site. The pastor wasn't comfortable with having a deacon and had other issues but still, I preached twice a month and officiated at weddings, marriage counseling, funerals, wake services, and annulments. I also distributed the Eucharist to shut-ins, and folks in nursing homes. One wedding was for two very poor young people whom I saw gathering Plumeria flowers in the churchyard for the bride and groom to wear as leis and their music was played from large boom-box CDs. No family of either bride or groom attended the ceremony. Most of the couples who came to be married were living together and some already had children as this couple did. I did not Judge them or scold them but told them that they were doing the right thing by getting married in the church and that their parents and grandparents were proud of them and so was God. I did one wedding on the beach at a home that was very elegant and where the bride wore a typical very expensive beautiful white wedding dress and the groom wore a tux, but both were barefooted. Only in Hawaii! I tried to get involved with the retreats that the Benedictines were conducting but was not encouraged to help, so I gave up that idea.

God closes some doors but opens others.

When we first came back to Hawaii, we often went to the Ilikai Hotel which was fairly new, and because they always had good Local Hawaiian entertainment and excellent food in the eating establishment called "The Top of the Ilikai." One night we were sitting at the bar, relaxing and I struck up a conversation with a guy who looked sad and lonely sitting next to me. He eventually told me what was bothering him. He had been and was still an undercover agent for the CIA and he and his partner and friend were discovered by the bad guys. They were attacked with knives and luckily he got away but his partner was killed. He was being brought home to Langley in Washington D.C. to be debriefed and was afraid that he was going to be fired or worse put in prison for the people he had killed in Thailand, while undercover and losing his partner. I think he was depressed, scared and sad that his friend was dead. He said it was his fault because he couldn't protect his friend when he needed him. I told him that he should just tell the truth when he got back to the mainland (the States) and he would be okay. I left him at the bar not long after that and have often wondered what happened to him and where he is now.

I will send people to you.

Also, while we were living in Hawaii and still on active duty, I heard that my New Jersey dentist shipmate Paul Farrell was selected for the rank of Admiral and as the new Inspector General, who was due to visit the Naval Dental Center facilities in Hawaii. I was excited to see

Paul again. When he finally arrived, he was so booked up during the day with his inspection business and social gatherings at night, that the only day he had free was Sunday. Luci and I had planned to go to a charismatic mass at St. Anthony's in Kailua that Sunday and I asked Paul to join us at the mass and lunch afterwards. I was very fearful, that Paul would think I had lost my marbles by attending such wild and charismatic service, but I prayed he would understand since he was raised as a very conservative Catholic in the Philadelphia area.

We arrived early for the mass and fortunately got seats and just sat and observed the people praising God with song, dancing in the aisles, and calling out praise to His name. All of this occurred before Mass started. The Mass was beautiful, lasted two hours, and you could feel the electricity in the air. The kiss of peace lasted 30 minutes and all this time I was afraid to look at Paul. The mass went on with constant celebration not only by the people in the pews and the isle but also by the priest and altar servers.

After we received communion, I finally dared to look at Paul and he had tears running down his face and he was glowing with joy. I was so relieved and happy. It was Paul's first exposure to the Charismatic Renewal, and he was just blown away and thanked me and Luci profusely for taking him and he said that he wanted to spend the rest of the day and evening learning about the renewal. I prayed over him to receive the gifts of the Holy Spirit and I found out later that he received the gifts of tongues the following week after he got back home. I went to his retirement ceremony 3 years later at the Navy Yard in Washington D.C. and you could tell by his reference to God in his farewell speech that he was still on fire with the Holy Spirit. He passed away about three years later in his home in Virginia Beach, Virginia and I thank God for having him in my life. His son, Paul Jr. became a Medical Doctor and made a career in the Navy Medical Corps. Paul's wife, Romaine, had been a Navy nurse when she and Paul met.

Chapter 39

Benedictine Monastery

Sometime after we returned to Hawaii, I ran into Peter Bahrans in 1986 at the Benedictine Monastery, whom I had previously known before we went back to Minnesota. After a long talk, he asked me if I would be his Spiritual Advisor. I agreed to do this with plans to meet once a month. Peter had a good job as a manager of a condominium complex in Hawaii Kai with a small crew to do maintenance work and various jobs. His job included a free 2-bedroom apartment. I did not know he was already abusing alcohol.

Peter asked me if it was a good idea to go to the Philippines and find someone to marry. I said no, I didn't think it was a good idea, because marriage should be based on love between a man and a woman. I told Peter that I would talk to my spiritual director, Fr. John Chandler, a Jesuit priest assigned to the Neuman Center, also called the Holy Spirit Parish. I told Fr. Chandler I thought it was a bad idea for many obvious reasons, but he responded by saying "Every man who desires to be married should not be held back despite the circumstances in meeting a willing woman."

Is that a celibate priest talking about getting married?

I explained that if a Philippina woman, who often lived in poverty could find a man willing to marry them, they would automatically become eligible to become a U.S. citizen and this was an important reason for them to marry anyone whom they might not love. I learned when I was in the Philippines on the USS New Jersey that this was a common way these women were able to escape poverty and eventually send money to their family members. They could then also be a sponsor for those who wanted to come to the United States after them, including their parents and siblings and anyone else. In my opinion, this was not the right reason for marriage. This wasn't love and was opposed to all moral tenets.

Fr. Chandler, however, stuck to his opinion, so I relented and told Peter he had permission to go to the Philippines to find a bride, which he did. He met her on the street. He and Malissa were married in the Catholic Church in downtown Manilla and honeymooned in Manilla in a hotel. During their stay, he took a picture of his new bride nude from the waist up and sent it to me.

I thought this was an early and very bad sign.

Well, they made it back to Hawaii and Malissa became pregnant soon after. They had a boy who they named David and later a girl who they named Maria. In the meantime, Peter was working at his condo management job. He was drinking heavier now and was becoming paranoid about many things, including having to report his progress to the Condominium Board of

Directors. Eventually, he was caught drinking on the job more than once and after many warnings he was fired.

Afterwards, the family moved into a condo on Ala Wai Blvd which belonged to a friend. Malissa in the meantime had gone to school and after getting her Nurses Aid certificate, started working. She eventually was working two jobs and wasn't home to take care of her children, or to be with Peter. Peter called me many times at night to take him to the emergency room or to a rehab center because of his abusive drinking.

He spent three treatments in long-care programs that I can remember and as soon as he graduated, he went right back to drinking. By now he was a full-fledged alcoholic. No matter what I did or said to him, he kept drowning himself in alcohol. One time he called me and said he was in a field crawling near the Monastery in a plowed field, drunk and out of control. I refused to come and get him, since I was in town and it was one o'clock in the morning. I learned later that he called Fr. David at the monastery, who came down and found him and got Peter into bed at the Monastery.

That morning, Fr. David caught Peter masturbating in the shower. He put Peter on a bus and sent him on his way back to Honolulu. All this time I had been communicating daily with Peter on the phone and often in person. Peter had another brilliant idea and thought that leaving Hawaii would make things better for him to go to Texas to live with his brother Richard, which he did.

Eventually, Richard's wife was fed up with Peter because he kept drinking, lying and creating problems for them and their marriage. Finally, Peter was asked to leave. He became homeless now in Texas. Peter got mugged and robbed more than once and ended up in a psych ward in a local hospital. He had no money and no food. He was arrested twice for vagrancy.

Once again, he called his brother Richard and received money to get a flight back to Hawaii. After many doctor appointments and a series of rehab facilities, psych wards, and homeless nights he was diagnosed with schizophrenic bi-polar manic depression syndrome. A case worker arranged to get Peter State welfare funds which amounted to $1,600.00 per month.

Now, Peter could pay his rent of $1,150.00 for a large studio apartment and then he planned to get food from various outreach programs and have $450.00 to spend on booze. I don't know how many times I rescued Peter and got him in the emergency room, short and long-term rehab programs and simply spent the time with him getting him safely home and in bed. Recently this recent year, 2022, I took Peter out to lunch and during the meal, he admitted to me that he did not get any COVID shots and didn't plan to.

I told him I would not see him or talk or text again until he got his two vaccinations and the two boosters. I meant it. In the meantime, he got a serious flesh-eating Staphylococcus infection in his right elbow from a fall on his moped and a broken spinal bone in the lumbar region of his back. He needed back surgery and the surgeon would not do the surgery until his elbow healed and he got all his COVID shots. He obeyed the doctor and eventually his elbow infection cleared up after a skin graft transplant from his back to his elbow and after completing his Covid series he had a Platinum plate attached to his spine with 6 screws on each side to hold it in place. This all took over two years to accomplish and during that time Peter finally woke up and quit drinking. He had his second sobriety anniversary which I attended with him at an AA meeting at Kapiolani Park on June 22, 2022, the Solemnity of the Saints Peter and Paul in the Catholic Liturgical calendar, his Patron Saints.

After nearly 40 years of traveling with Peter and holding his hand in his drunken journey, Peter is whole and still healing, and on his way to being a sober human Being.

God heals and forgives us all!

***

Two weeks after his anniversary, however, he fell off the wagon and drank. He said he wanted one more encounter with alcohol before he quit forever. Of course, that was a lie that the evil one told him, and he believed it. He said he was very sick the next day. So, we are starting over after thirty-eight years of effort.

Peter is now on and off the wagon and it seems hopeless again.

I'm still walking with Peter, holding his hand and trusting in God's all-merciful Grace. In the midst of this darkness, I still hold on to my faith and that God will heal him and forgive him.

***

Luci and I took a month off (I had leave accumulated from the Navy) and went to Tonga to do dentistry for the people there. We had a letter of introduction for Dr. John Felix who was the head of the International Red Cross to the Queen of Tonga asking for hospitality for our attempt to give free dentistry to the people. We also had a Tongan Catholic Sister who would guide us to the different villages where she knew help was needed. There were no dental offices to work in, so we worked on lanais or under a tree. The village leader always presented himself first for treatment, which was basic cleaning, extractions, and oral hygiene instructions with a gift of a toothbrush and paste and floss.

I was known as "Nifo Dokata" (tooth doctor). There were two Tongan dentists in a clinic in the capital city of Nuku'alofa but they expect the people to come to them with their oral needs. Most of them didn't. Luci also took blood pressure readings, heart rate, and estimated weight of the adults. I remember the women averaged 200 pounds and the men 220 pounds. I found rampant decay among the children due to the diet changing from protein, primarily fish, to carbohydrates in the form of candy and soda pop brought in by Western influence. We were given a feast by many families we helped and were able to go to daily mass in the church near the Queen Salo'te pier. The Tongan singing and horn playing were always so beautiful and inspiring. One day at mass it was really hot in the church as it usually was. No air conditioning. A Tongan lady sitting next to me was fanning herself with a fan that was obviously handmade, and she started fanning me. I looked her with a big smile and said "Thank You" a few minutes she returned to fanning herself. So typical of the Tongan people. Kind and generous with a smile on her face. We did meet the Queen and she asked us if we could bring young Tongan girls to Hawaii to train as dental assistants, Kind of like a nurses-aid. We said we would try but on arriving back to Hawaii and consulting with many others, we found that the logistics were impossible to overcome. Nowhere to train them and no place to live and no funds available. I did, however, write an article on our dental experiences in Tonga and it was published in the Journal of the Hawaii Association, July 1980, Vol X1, Number 2.

I also went on a Medical and Dental mission with the Hawaii Medical Fellowship Foundation whose founder was Dr. John Seah, a friend of mine through meeting many times at the Benedictine Monastery of Hawaii. The same man who I mentioned previously from Singapore who got his medical training in Ireland and married an Irish girl. Our mission was to go to an Orphanage in Guangzhou, Canton, China from March 17 to 27, 1994 to do volunteer Medical and Dental treatment for the children that were housed there who experienced little medical or dental care. I was the only Dentist, and I took Tran my Vietnamese dental assistant from the Hawaii Family Dental Centers. We also had two plastic surgeons (for hair lip reconstruction), one orthopedic surgeon, Dr. Larry Gordon, one general practitioner, two pediatricians including Dr. Amy Jacang, and two nurses.

We also picked up an interpreter for me in Hong Kong, who I used extensively during our stay. We also visited two married dentists who I had worked with in Hawaii, who had moved to Hong Kong to set up practice. To their surprise, most of their patients were Japanese and they had to learn the Japanese language quickly. They had a beautiful dental office.

We took a train from Hong Kong to Guangzhou, had lunch on the train and Tran commented that the countryside looked just like home in Vietnam. We stayed in separate rooms at the Garden Hotel, a five-star hotel in the center of the city. The lobby was two football fields long and at least 50 yards wide. I contained a 10-foot long and tall sail boat all made from jade and other museum-type art pieces were displayed on this massive lobby. Their breakfast buffet was the largest buffet I have ever seen and 50% Western food of all kinds. The people in the city mostly walked or rode a bicycle. There were very few cars, but those were high-end cars such as BMW, Mercedes Benz, or Bentleys.

We had a chance to tour the city and its many parks business centers, hospitals, and retirement centers. There were street vendors everywhere selling goods such as fruits, vegetables, fish, live eels, live or butchered fowl, and spices. We also visited one nursing home which seemed more of a retirement center for people with money. We also visited a modern hospital that was full of wealthy patients. I discovered a side entrance and learned that was where the poor people entered the hospital for care. I went in and discovered that it was a multi-step down in quality of furnishings and upkeep. It was filthy. I was disappointed and wondered what else they were hiding from us.

Our hosts kept treating us to tours and nine-course dinners as the days slipped by. I told my interpreter that I thought the Chinese were embarrassed by our presence and were "losing face" because we were going to do what they should be doing ie: taking care of their young orphans. I told her that I had enough tours and dinners and I wanted to go to the orphanage and begin helping the children. We left the next day in a van and the other members of the Medical Team came two days later. I learned that the plastic surgeons were not given any hair lip patients and the Orthopedic Surgeon had only one surgery and that was in the wealthy side of the hospital and not at the orphanage. The orphanage was a one-hour drive into the country.

When we arrived, I was told that I had to treat the staff of the orphanage first and the children later. I told them through my interpreter that I would see the children first in the morning and the staff in the afternoon or we would leave. They agreed. Tran and I worked 8 to 10 hours each day and were served Lunch in a local country café. The children were brave. I discovered a small room that contained small boxes, each containing a baby wrapped very tight in a wool blanket. I was told they were given a bottle of milk and it was only propped up not fed to them by a person. If the bottle slipped out of the child's mouth that was too bad, it was not replaced. If the baby didn't cry it was not fed at all. It would die of starvation. So cruel and so sad. We stopped for lunch and were taken to a small country café. I noticed wicker baskets outside the front door of the café and looked inside one of the baskets and discovered a multiple variety of live snails, all in shells, which were to be served as part of our lunch. I also noticed the chopsticks we were to use were on the table were sitting in a jar of tea. I wondered if that was their way of sanitizing their utensils. I was hungry and the food was okay, and I used their chopsticks.

We treated many children in the seven days that we were in the orphanage. We had forgotten to bring needles, syringes, and capsules of Novocain, so we had to scrounge a large needle and syringes and a bottle of Novocain. Those shots must have hurt but most of the children were very brave and appreciative of our efforts to help them. On the last day there a male staff member asked if we would treat his son. We agreed and the young boy was severely mentally retarded and we had to get help to hold him down while he screamed and kicked violently. He was making so much noise that Tran and I could barely communicate but we extracted a half dozen or more teeth and felt that we had done our best. God was good to us, and we returned home as changed people realizing there was much work to do in God's great world.

Chapter 40

Mililani

After two years at St Michael's in Waialua, the pastor was recalled into semi-retirement after I told our Bishop Francis X DiLorenzo about his several emotional and physical problems. He was always late starting mass just so he could smoke a cigarette before mass. He also had a drinking problem and didn't want to do weddings or funerals followed by the internment.

The pastor also made up a different statement during the consecration which I thought devaluated and nullified the mass. After the pastor was moved, I requested to be transferred to St. John, the Apostle and Evangelist Church in Mililani town. Father Gordian Carvalho was the pastor there.

I remember just a few days before my first homily at St. John's. Fr. Gordy was reluctant to let me preach. I said:

"Why don't you want me to preach?

Fr Gordy said:

"It's an important Sunday"

My response was:

"They are all important."

I preached that Sunday and all masses I was assigned to during my time there as Deacon. I think Fr. Gordy thought my homilies were good. He never had doubts after that. I mostly only preached there once a month because the Hope Alive Counseling was enough to keep me busy.

I recruited a lady parishioner to assist Luci and I in our Hope Alive counseling. She worked out very well. Eventually however, I was reassigned to Our Lady of Peace Cathedral in downtown Honolulu.

This came about primarily because we had moved to Harbor Court in town across from the Aloha Marketplace and I could walk to the Cathedral in 6 minutes.

During my time at the Cathedral, many personalities conflicted and clashed with each other, and I left to Join Father Carvalho again. At his request, I was transferred to the Sacred Heart Church near Punahou School the same day that he was transferred there from St. John's. We became good friends over the months and years and Luci, and I shared dinner often with him at various restaurants. We served two churches, Sacred Heart near Punahou and Pius X in Manoa, and was staffed by two priests and two deacons, I was one of them.

Chapter 41

Other Important Stories

I realized that God was still sending people to me. But now there was a church full of people in the pews and I was able to share my thoughts about His Son two or three times each month during Mass and Baptisms. I was so always very serious about my monthly homilies because I was able to talk about His Son, Jesus and by the words I spoke, draw people to a closer relationship with Him. Even at baptisms I had to tell those happy parents, relatives and friends (who were often not Catholic) about His Son Jesus.

***

Friends of my parents, Norbert (Nubs) and Patty Furth, from Faribault, Minnesota, now lived in Honolulu in the Wailana condo building near the Hilton Hawaiian Village. Luci and I also became friends with them. They were also Catholic. We lived about three blocks from them and were invited to dinner a few times to enjoy a Minnesota pot roast dinner, finished off with homemade apple pie ala mode. Patty was an excellent cook and welcoming hostess. She had a custom drapery business, and Nubs was a commercial and private painter. They both worked on my parent's new home on Roberds Lake. Patty made all the draperies and Nubs did all the painting.

Eventually Nubs, who was addicted to smoking cigarettes, was dying from lung cancer and the local hospice was coming to help Patty take care of his needs. I also came daily for about two weeks and prayed the rosary with Nubs. He didn't join me in prayer, just listened intently. The day before he passed, he told me about a visitor he had. He saw a beautiful lady who was near him and felt very peaceful. I asked him if she said anything and he said, "No, she just smiled."

I asked him if he knew who the lady was, and he said "Mary." He died that night in his bed. I took her appearance as a blessing and as a sign of accompaniment with Nubs to Heaven. Some people die so peacefully like Nubs did.

***

Somehow, after eventually returning to Hawaii, I don't remember how I met a Byzantine priest from Canada who was studying for a PhD in religious studies at the University of Hawaii. He was living in a small cottage on the St. Francis High school campus. For some reason he came into disfavor with the Catholic Bishop in Hawaii and was evicted from the cottage and expelled from the University.

He was homeless when I met him. I invited him to live with us, which he accepted with sincere gratitude, until he could get his life back together. He stayed for about three weeks. When he left, he gave us gifts that he had acquired in his travels around the Middle East and Europe. The most precious is a first-class relic of St. Peter, a tiny bit of bone found under the altar at St. Peter's

100

Basilica in Rome where St. Peter was buried. I wonder about its authenticity sometimes. The second gift was a wooden mosaic depicting one of the ten lepers that Jesus cured, but the only one who returned to thank Jesus. The leper was shown as deeply bowing to Jesus in thanksgiving for being cured. Each wooden peace of the mosaic was a different type of wood, making the colors of the artwork very beautiful and skillfully assembled. He gave us other small gifts besides these two. After we transported him to the airport to leave Hawaii, we never heard from him again.

***

One of the projects that I did in between patients in my dental practice, was to call all Catholic Churches, Catholic religious centers, Catholic Schools and Monasteries to suggest to them that they and their members should set aside either a daily or weekly time to pray for all life issues, including before birth (abortions) and before death (assisted suicide) and all life issues in between. Most of them agreed to do that. I made some on site visits, including St. John's the Apostle and Evangelist in Mililani. Fr. Gary Secor was the pastor at that time. I remember his comment concerning my ideas about starting a plan to pray for all life issues.

He said:

"I am a priest, and I should be doing what you are doing. I'm very impressed by your efforts to preserve life. Thank you for lighting a fire under me."

***

Out of the hundreds of homilies that I did in Hawaii and in Minnesota, one really stands out in my mind. As I prepared to preach at Sacred Heart Church in lower Manoa, Honolulu, I decided to stage a talk with my Grand Mother Anna concerning life issues in her younger years and now. I used a rocking chair as a prop and told the congregation to imagine my Grand Mother rocking and listening to me.

I used four stories based on the things that she had told me:

The first story began with me asking, *"Grandma, do you remember when you used to hook up the horse and buggy in the Winter with skids instead of wheels because of the deep snow and you would take the Doctor out into the country to deliver babies? Grandma, did you know now, that mothers kill their babies before they are born. This is called Abortion."*

Grandma's response was:

"Oh, Jesus please forgive us."

Before I could go any further, I noticed the dead, piercing silence in the church. You could hear a pin drop.

The second story began thus:

101

"Grandma, do you remember when your extended family all pitched in when the oldest family member got too old to help himself or herself with things, they couldn't do anymore? Now, a doctor gives a fatal dose of medicine to the old person so that they die the same day, and the family does not stop this terrible deed. Grandma, this is called Assisted Suicide."

I could hear someone crying in the church. Grandma's response was:

'Oh, Sweet Jesus, Have mercy on us."

There was still the same, dead silence.

The third story started with me asking:

"Grandma, did you know that the people who murder others in peace time is happening 400% more often than when you were a young girl."

She responded:

"Oh my God, what is this world coming to?"

As far as the fourth story is concerned, for the life of me, I cannot remember it and all my notes are long gone. Oh well. I suppose that's life; not always perfect, but at least you get the idea that I was preaching about one the most important issues in my life and that issue was the LIFE given to us by God.

Chapter 42

Problem Pregnancy Center

I think it was around 2006, I was visiting a Problem Pregnancy Center to pick up some "life issues" pamphlets and during that visit I was given a fetus in a jar of formaldehyde. I was told that the fetus was 7 months in utero when aborted. It was a totally intact, preserved little boy. I promised that I would bury the child soon. My first thought was I could just bury it in an unmarked grave at the Catholic Cemetery on King Street. I called the facilities director of the Catholic Diocese and was told that there were no more burials allowed there because there were already many unmarked graves and there was no record of where these were buried.

He also explained to me that all the records were kept in a small wooden building and years ago it burned to the ground and all the records were destroyed. I was discouraged and the baby stayed in my home for months and I was wondering what to do. I eventually called Father David Barfknecht the Superior at the Benediction Monastery and asked him if I could bury the baby in the hills above the Monastery at a location called the Grotto, where people came to pray before a small statue of the Blessed Mother. He agreed and we met a few days later.

At the grotto, I dug a small grave just below the statue of Mary, removed the baby from the jar and wrapped it in a purificator from the alter at the monastery chapel. Father David and I recited an internment prayer from the Book of Funerals, blessed the baby with holy water and buried it. I placed small stones around edge of the burial plot, and we left. I have not been back since, but I know that this innocent child is in the arms of Jesus and enjoying the Beatific Vision of God and His Angels and Saints.

"Bring the children to me."

Chapter 43

Cruises

Luci and I took many ocean-liner cruises while we were still young and healthy. We also took a few land trips to countries like to Israel, France, Ireland, Great Britain, Australia, and New Zealand Athens and Santorini, Greece. Concerning our cruises, I don't think we used the same cruise line more than twice. We cruised on the Princes Line twice, the Holland Line twice, the Conard Line once, a small cruise ship (25 state rooms) that went to the Great Barrier Reef off the coast of Australia for scuba diving the Great Barrier Reef; a river cruise down the Nile River in Egypt, staying overnight in the Sheraton, in Cairo, Egypt, ending at Aswan dam near the ancient city of Luxor, the temple of many Pharaohs.

We also took many other day tours offered by the cruise lines and enjoyed the many different cultures, architecture, cuisine, people and customs of different countries. We visited Sweden, Oslo Norway, the town Christiansen, where the Nelsons immigrated from to the US (including a cruise down the fjords and a helicopter ride and landing on an iceberg in Norway} and Copenhagen, Denmark. I noticed that the Danes had the most obvious and extreme Scandinavian accent. We also had a short visit to St. Petersburg, Russia. We cruised the Black Sea after a day tour of Istanbul Turkey where we saw the great Muslim Mosques which had previously been Catholic Cathedrals. The ocean channel there at Istanbul divides the European countries from the Asian countries.

We made stops in Bulgaria, Romania, Russia, Georgia and Ukraine while in the Black Sea. We did more than one cruise in the Mediterranean. Enjoying Rome twice, where we visited the Church of St. Francis of Rome my patroness Saint. Her relics are encased in a glass box under the main altar in the church. Also visited Athens and Santorini, Greece. One land tour was to Czechoslovakia, where we spent time with relatives of Grandma Anna Lund.

Luci and I enjoyed wandering in a rental car so much that we decided to tour France and see the Catholic Cathedrals famous in France. Our first stop was Notre Dame de Paris, which we had seen before, but is was still a beautiful monument to the faith of mankind and to the Mother of God. We snuck in a tour of the Louvre, which now had a glass pyramid as one of its main entrances. I wanted to see the Mona Lisa. From there we drove and went to Monte St. Michael for the second time but stayed in a small boutique hotel overnight. From there we went to the Basilica of De Lisieux, Where St. Teresa, the Little Flower is entombed. Finally, to Notre Dame de Reims and Notre Dame de Chartres and last to Notre Dame de Nevers where St Bernadette is displayed in a non-corrupt location near the main alter of the church. I was amazed at the great efforts the people of France to build these magnificent edifices to God and His Mother and which took centuries to build. Every important story of the Holy Scripture was told in the stain glass windows of Chartres. Even the floors are decorated magnificently with a maze at the entrance of Chartres.

***

Another Mediterranean cruise took us down the Suez Canal where our first stop was in Jordon. On the way there we spotted lone military type men periodically stationed along the upper sandy banks on the Jordon side with machine guns, watching us very closely. We took a bus trip to Amman escorted front and back by jeeps with mounted 50 caliber guns always manned. In Amman we found very few people and found out that day was some sort of holiday (probably Ramadan) since most shops were closed. Without much to do we got some picnic lunch and settled down in a small park. There were two ladies sitting near us and their two boys were kicking a soccer ball around. I joined the boys, and we had a three-way soccer kicking fun time. Their mothers were chatting and smoking on a single Hakka pipe. I asked them if it was for tobacco, but they said it was only mint flavored.

I asked if I could try it and after they said yes. I took a small inhale drag and found it to be pleasant. They said their husbands were in the military and were gone on some kind of assignment. We also visited the ancient city of Petra which was carved out of sandstone in the 5th century BC as well as the huge King Abdullah Mosque. From there, we continued our cruise past Abu Dhabi and the UAE and finally stopped in Dubai. We left our cruise ship there and spent a few days in a hotel, which turned out to be the oldest hotel in Dubai and it was only 14 years old. We had many great adventures there. We had lunch one day in the Burj Khalifa, a 380 meter (Approximately 114 stories) high hotel and resort on the ocean shaped like a sail. I skied on snow at an indoor ski facility attached to the main mall shopping center which had a snow mountain to ski on, department stores and an indoor ice-skating rink. Luci sat and watched me ski from a restaurant at the foot of the slope.

It was a long ski down considering it was indoors. About equal to a hill ski resort in Minnesota. We also visited a bar all constructed totally of blocks of Ice. It was about 10 degrees below zero inside and they provided us with heavy duty parkas, gloves and watch caps. For some reason the glasses in which the drinks were served did not stick to your lips. The stools, couches and all furniture were made of ice. We took a trip out to a Bedouin village in the desert and toured a camel riding race as well as a falcon hunting exhibition. Later, in the evening we were led to large open tents and served Bedouin food and were entertained by belly dancers. In Dubai there was construction going on everywhere. I was told that 25% of all cranes in the world were in Dubai.at that time. From our hotel window I could count fourteen cranes. The thousands of construction workers came from many poor countries and were paid minimum wages to work 12 hours seven days a week and were given free room and board in temporary villages.

They sent most of their money home to support friends and family.

Chapter 44

St. Mary's

I eventually retired as a Deacon in September 2019, the same time that Father Gordy retired and moved to Las Vegas, Nevada. I didn't take him long to miss Hawaii and his friends and doctors. He came back two years later. He had lost weight by eating less and walking 6 days a week for 45 minutes in the Ala Moana Shopping Center. We now meet for lunch monthly and reminisce and chit-chat. We never seem to run out of things to discuss.

It didn't take long for me to realize that I missed my deacon efforts, especially the preaching and sharing of the story of Jesus and how he knocked on the door of everyone's heart. I thought a lot about what to do about the empty void in my heart, which seemed to grow stronger by the day.

I started by looking in the Phone Book under "Churches" and I found an Episcopal Church named St. Mary's. I thought that was odd, since I knew that few if any non-Catholic denominations had much to do with the Blessed Mother, especially to dedicate a church name to Her. I was drawn there by Mary's name. The small church was close near home on South King Street, so we decided to go to their only service on Sunday at 9 am. It was a very small community comprising some 80+ souls. It also had a small 100-year-old chapel adjoining but not attached to the main church. This was the original St Mary's. There was a beautiful garden and statue of the Blessed Mother between the old chapel and the main church.

One of the church's original parishioners was Danial Kahikina Inouye, who was a longtime senator in the United States Senate. Father Gregory Johnson, who was the pastor had named the chapel "Soldiers Chapel," since the funds to build it came from a retired Civil War General. It was being used by a small Episcopal Korean community which also had only one service on Sunday morning. The pastor of St. Mary's, Father Johnson, was an ordained Episcopal Minister, a former Airforce Chaplain, a former Professor of religious studies at the University of Hawaii, and a native of Stillwater Minnesota.

I was so impressed that God had led me to another Norwegian from Minnesota who loved God and Blessed Mother as much as I did. It was a wonderful connection, since Luci and I were both from Faribault Minnesota. He was a very friendly and enthusiastic man of his small flock and celebrated the mass with deep feelings, especially during the Eucharistic Consecration. They served brunch after mass every Sunday in the attached hall. Father Gregory was a very loving shepherd towards his small flock. We liked the whole concept and atmosphere and after the third week mass in attendance we met with Fr. Gregory and asked him if he would like to have me serve St. Mary's as a deacon. He said yes and a new adventure had begun.

Yes, I was allowed to preach often and felt very close to the community and to Father Gregory in a very short time. A homeless lady named "Rosey" was a special gift from God and in my mind and was a symbol of the Love reaching out from St. Mary's Church to those in need. I was able to get a new roof on "Soldiers Chapel" and encouraged a church member to write a grant to get new wiring installed also in the Solder's Chapel. The wiring was completed one year later. There were many outreach efforts and activities to attend and be involved in including the homeless on the site; more efforts in outreach than I have ever seen accomplished in any church in my experience, and I was delighted to be able to participate in a few of them.

My preaching was different in that I was more focused on the Gospel lesson and how we could apply it to our lives and less on "calling the people to Christ." I am sure that this "calling" theme was still deeply threaded into the words of my homilies anyway. After one year Father Gregory retired and so did I, again. We have become close friends and meet often to share a meal and stories. Over the weeks and months that we met, I had started telling him the many "God moments" that I had experienced in my life. I considered this a gift from God to extend my Diaconate service in the small Episcopal community and I no longer had an empty void in my heart.

***

I suddenly realized that I had nothing to do again, so I joined the American Legion, Post 1 in Honolulu. I volunteered to be the Post Chaplain in which capacity I served for 2 years. In the 3rd year, I was elected Commander of the Post and have been in that position for 7 years. It's just another position God has given to me to carry on His work only this time with helping and encouraging Veterans and others on active duty.

We do many events each year including placing miniature flags at the graves of Veterans at Oahu Cemetery on Memorial Day, marching in a Veteran's Parade on Veterans Day, constructing and installing a large (16' X 5'0) Walls of Honor at two Plaza nursing homes and more to come. We emphasized "You will never be forgotten" to those resident veterans and honored JROTC High School Cadets with medals and ribbons at their annual banquet. We are in the process of hosting sailors from the Pearl Harbor Sub-Base to our homes so those whose sailors families who are not in Hawaii could experience a family meal at Thanksgiving. We also had guest speakers to update us on many subjects including benefits and injury compensation such as the Pact-Act, Suicide prevention in the military and supporting the local Wounded Warriors Ohana and the Society of Purple Heart veterans. We also have a Christmas party for our members and their spouses. Santa always shows up.

Chapter 45

Sickness

As the years passed by, Luci's diabetes slowly got worse.

One morning when she was in the bathroom, I noticed the big toe on her right foot was darker than the others. Upon closer inspection, the front part of her toe was black. She had problems with her toenails curling in at the edges and growing into the skin on both sides of the nail. I immediately thought of gangrene. After breakfast, I took her to the ER at Straub Hospital, and they agreed that her toe was gangrenous. They contacted a vascular surgeon from Straub, Dr. Elna Masuda and the next day later she amputated Luci's toe. Unfortunately, the infection had already traveled to the second toe, and surgery was planned for the next day.

After a few days of recovery, it appeared that the other three toes were also infected so Luci had to be put back in surgery. The third time. She now had all five of her toes on her right foot amputated. A few weeks went by, and Dr. Masuda determined after an echo that Luci's leg veins were not supplying enough return blood to help the leg fight more infection. She had three more surgeries to put in stents and bypasses in both of her legs. That was 6. A few months later, she developed gangrene in the toes of her left foot, and it was progressing very fast. Dr. Masuda gave Luci two options:

1. to amputate all toes on her left foot or,

2. Amputate her left foot above the ankle.

Luci chose the first option and went back into surgery. That was #7. She recovered fast and the gangrene didn't progress any further. While she was learning to walk with no toes after rehab and practice at home, she started developing large ulcers on the soles of her right and left foot despite being on antibiotics for months.

Dr. Brian Pien, an Infectious Disease specialist was watching that persistent problem as well as prescribing her antibiotics which she took for months on end. I also took Luci twice weekly for visits to the Wound Clinic at Queen's Hospital. In addition, Luci was also seen bi-monthly by a podiatrist surgeon attached to the Queen's Hospital. It seemed like all we did was go to doctor appointments for a couple of years. I also had to take Luci to the beauty shop monthly for washing, set, and style, nail appointments, grocery shopping, cooking, and cleaning. There were also prescription call-ins and pick-ups at Pearl Harbor pharmacy, blood sugar tests 4 times a day, and insulin shots four times a day.

Twice she had a "PIC" inserted in a blood vessel in her arm to give her IV antibiotics directly into her bloodstream which I did. We took a daily drive to Ala Moana Park, after I got her an ice cream cone at Burger King, so she could get fresh air and read from her Apple tablet. I usually fell asleep while she was reading.

I was getting tired. At one point early in this process, my mother and Luci were both in the Straub Hospital. The emergency Doctor asked me if I was alright with this multiple caregiving I was providing.

I told him that I had tightness in my chest often and they did some tests and told me that my main problem was stress. I said, sarcastically to that, "No kidding!"

Luci's heart was giving her problems and after consultations with Cardiac doctors at Straub Hospital she was scheduled for open heart surgery to replace a valve and place a stent. Surgery #8.

At this point, I knew that I was heading for a physical breakdown myself.

Within a month, my mother went to a hospice care center and passed away in three days. I sent her body back to Minnesota to be buried next to my dad in the Blooming Prairie, Minnesota cemetery.

After Luci was able to come home, she had difficulty walking because her toes were now gone and fell many times trying to get around. During this time prior, we had my mother Mimi with us, and she had her own medical needs due to her age. And I was trying to take of both of them. I was getting sick myself.

Chapter 46

New Beginnings

Sometime in 2009, I realized that Luci and I had not been intimate for over 7 years. I was tired of releasing myself of sexual tension, so I decided to look for intimacy elsewhere.

Dear God help me!

I went to different places and was satisfied physically but not emotionally. After longing for something more, I finally found I Nam, who had her own business. I kept coming back because I realized that despite her anger and drinking issues, she had a good heart, and I was so lonesome and unhappy. I realized that at her core, she was a good person, and that she had good reasons to have these issues because selling herself was not making her happy and was self-degrading. I stayed with her when she prepared dinner a few times, but she often drank too much beer and cried a lot.

She either lamented the loss of her husband to divorce in her early life and failure and often called one of her sisters in Korea and cried on the phone to them. She went home to Korea about every two or three years and tried to make up for leaving her family by buying her sisters expensive gifts from Gucci, Louis Vuitton and other high-end store products. She eventually moved her business closer to Waikiki and I continued to see her and tried to support her and other two girl employees.

Owing to the big turn down in the economy and her business she eventually had to sell it at a low price.

She and I had previously become partners in real estate investments. We were able to acquire and flip condos three times until we had significant equity value. She lived in these apartments that we bought and upgraded. I eventually sold my three condo units in Harbor Court and bought a beautiful ocean-view condo in the Moana Pacific complex where we started living together in the Fall of 2019.

With left over equity, we purchased a new Condo in the Azure condo building just two blocks away and paid off the Moana Pacific mortgage. After taking a low-level job in a 1-2-3 store and getting her Sciatic nerve injured from lifting a heavy case of soft drinks, I suggested that she find a better and safer position. I knew she was smart enough to start her own business. She decided she would like to go to Massage Therapy School but could not afford it. The school was a few blocks from where we lived so it was convenient. I paid for her tuition which was $6,000. After six months of school, she studied for another two months and took the State Board Exam and passed it the first time. Considering that her first language was Korean and her English reading skills were poor, she did remarkably well to pass the exam on her first try. She found a small, four-room, 2ⁿᵈ-floor space that had room for one massage table, which she had custom-made, one small bedroom, a kitchen, and a full bath.

She moved in, I had signs made leading to the entrance and the customers started coming immediately. She also advertised in the newspaper and that generated some customers. She works alone and now after nine years of practice, has garnered a hundred plus steady customers and makes a healthy six-figure income. She doesn't need to advertise any more.

I Nam and I took a few trips when Luci was either in the hospital or Sharon took care of her in Flagstaff Arizona. Our first trip was to South Korea to visit and meet her family, which consists of three sisters and a half dozen nieces. During this trip we took walks in the mountains, visited Buddhist temples, and many other interesting places including Jeju Island south of the mainland of Korea. We rode horseback once in Jeju Island and took the bus to most places there and in Soule We witnessed a fireworks show put on by Korea, Japan, and China and it was by far the most spectacular fireworks show I have ever witnessed. We took a second trip to visit her family a couple of years later. Her sister Oaksum worked as a cook in a restaurant and produced wonderful Korean meals for us at home.

We also took a week and went to Eli Minnesota to explore the North Boundary country and go fishing. I hired a fishing guide who had a boat with a radar, and we had no trouble catching fish. I Nam caught the largest Walleye.

Oh, was she excited!

The guide made a fish lunch with American Fries and beans on a small Island set up just for that cause. It even had a picnic table. Another trip was to Yellowstone Park, which included traveling in a luxury rental car from Salt Lake City, Utah, to Idaho Falls, Idaho (where I was stationed in the Navy) to Yellowstone Park where we stayed for three days and saw the whole park, including "Ole Faithful." Our final destination was a hot spring resort in Montana where we stayed for two days.

What a great trip.

It was all new to I Nam and she enjoyed the trip, especially seeing the buffalo, elk, mountain goats, the thick forests, rivers and of course "Old Faithful."

On our latest trip to Maui, we stayed at the Ka'annapali Resort. We got into the ocean every day, did lots of shopping and eating; relaxing however we could. As Luci and I aged, her health deteriorated due to severe diabetes. shots.

As a friend, I Nam Kim visited Mimi often at home and at her rehab times. She also took Mimi, Luci and me out for dinner often. Mimi slowly got very feeble and eventually ended up in Hospice. She died on January 19, 2010, at the age of 91. Luci was getting harder and harder to care for and keep her safe. I Nam now became friends with Luci. She would come to visit her at home and often cleaned the house for us. She also gave Luci haircuts, dyed her hair, and colored and filed her nails.

The three of us went out to dinner often and sometimes to the Elks club for dinner and dancing. Luci couldn't dance so I danced with I Nam. I was getting weaker physically now that I was in my early 80's. Luci was incontinent and was falling a lot, despite my asking her to use the walker, which she refused to do. I eventually had to place Luci in a Foster Care Home in Eva Beach under the care of Elsa Attis on April 22, 2019. There were only three clients in the Care Home and because of that low number, Luci gets a lot of one-on-one attention, which makes me feel very grateful. It costs a lot less than a nursing home at $6,000.00 a month vice $11,000.00 per month. That still adds up to $72,000.00 per year.

I had to hire a case worker company costing $525.00 per month. They come twice a month to check on Luci's care and well-being. This also added $6,300.00 more expense for Luci's care per year totaling $78,300.00 each year.

Indeed, God has provided.

Chapter 47

I Nam

During her first 64 years, I Nam remained a Buddhist follower and I went with her a few times to the temple to make offerings and prayer. She came one time to the Catholic mass to hear me preach. She told me that when she was younger and already in the United States, she would go to Catholic Mass with a girl-friend. She continued in Buddhism anyway. I eventually spoke to God about our living situation and my feelings. I offered her to God that someday she would accept Jesus into her life and become a Catholic. Sometime in May 2019, I started praying to St. Monica asking her to open I Nam's heart to Jesus just as she had prayed for her son St. Augustine to convert. In late 2021 she said yes in her heart and started taking RCIA classes at a local Korean Church. She was Baptized in that Church on Easter Sunday morning, April 17, 2022. She planned to continue going to that Korean Church, St. Andrew Kim Oratory and I will go to St Peter and Paul church nearby. Update: We are now going to St. Peter and Paul church together every Sunday to the 7 or 9 am mass. I Nam likes Fr. Kahn, the pastor who is a very holy man and priest.

I found out in late May 2022 that Father Michael Sawyer, the founder of the Benedictine Monastery of Hawaii, whose health was failing, was now in the St. Francis Hospice on Liliha Street. I called Sister MaryJo at the monastery inquiring as to the status of Father Michael and was told he was not doing well and was in and out of awareness. She said that she fed him the last time the community visited him because he couldn't do it himself. I realized that his birthday was coming up on April 11th and asked MaryJo if the community was going to join Father to celebrate his 97th Birthday.

She said the community had a function at the monastery to attend to and could not be there on the 11th. I told her that I would visit Him on the 11th. So, I did. When I arrived, he was sitting by the window in his wheelchair just staring at his lunch. I greeted him and we talked for a while. I asked him if he knew who I was, and he said yes, you are Ron. I asked him if I could help him with his lunch and he said yes, so I proceeded to feed him, and he ate almost all of it. He seemed to have some difficulty chewing (maybe had a bad tooth) but finally got most of it down. I then asked him if we wanted to say the rosary with me and he said yes and immediately pulled his rosary out of his pocket (he knew right where it was) and we started saying the joyful mysteries since it was Monday. I led and he responded. Father Michael nodded on and off a couple of times during the prayer, but we finished, and he put his rosary back in his pocket. Father Michael and I didn't say anything after saying the rosary and neither did he for 10 or 15 minutes and I realized he was tired, and it was time for me to go. I asked him to bless me and he made the sign of the cross on my forehead and blessed me in the name of the Father, the Son, and the Holy Spirit and said a beautiful prayer over me. He thanked me for coming to visit him and I left. Father Michael passed away 6 days later, on Easter Sunday morning. I have known Father Michael since 1974 when we first met at the Benedictine Monastery in Bennet Lake, Wisconsin, 46 years ago. I think I was the last one to visit him and I will never forget that short time with him.

RIP, my dear friend.

***

I remember I took a tour with friends from the monastery led by Father Michael. We had planned to go to Rome for the Canonization of Fr. Damien, but it was canceled when Pope John-Paul II broke his leg. We didn't change our schedule and decided to go anyway and visit as many Benedictine Monasteries as possible throughout France and Belgium. Our first stop was in Normandy France, where Fr. Michael had been in the military invasion on D-Day. He was in the second wave on that day and was wounded twice. We also went to the huge Normandy American Cemetery and started saying the Rosary among the thousands of tombstones.

As we prayed, everyone nearby came to join us in prayer. That was very touching. We visited many monasteries over the ten days and stayed overnight in most of them and were able to join the monks in their prayers and meals. One monastery made beer to raise money and it was the best beer I have ever tasted. The highlight for me was when we visited St. Benoit Monastery in Loiret, France which contains the remains of St. Benedict. His relics were in a simple black square wooden box with no extra adornment sitting in the middle of the crypt.

We also visited and toured Monte St. Michael Monastery in Normandy, where Luci and I had also visited previously.

Chapter 48

Luci, Mom and I Nam

Much to my surprise, during one of my mom's rehab stays, I entered my mom's room and found I Nam sitting there with my mom. Once, during our conversations, I had vaguely mentioned that my mom was in a rehab facility. I noticed that my mom was all smiles and even laughing a bit. I Nam told me she loved old people and wanted to visit my mom often. After her rehab, I Nam came to visit Mom often at her home, in the same condo building, Harbor Court, where Luci and I lived. She also took my mom and Luci out to dinner many times and Mom always got excited to get all dressed up for the occasion. As I got to know I Nam, I soon recognized that she had a special love for the elderly. Eventually, my mother got so weak that she had to go into a hospice. But in the meantime, I Nam visited Luci often, giving her shampoos and haircut, dying and styling. One time she took over for me and finished cutting her toenails. She also trimmed and polished her fingernails. The three of us spent many at dinner and dancing at the Elks club and other great restaurants. Luci always wanted Crab Cakes if they were on the menu.

In desperation for my own health, I put Luci in daycare Center for about a year and later tried to get paid help to come into our home, to give me a break but I was not happy with the quality of people the agency sent. I finally contacted Catholic Charities and they referred me to a case worker company in Pearl City who then referred me to a Foster Care Home. In Ewa Beach. I felt like I was at my wit's end as well as exhausted but decided to check out this referral. I had heard many horror stories about poor care, abuse, and neglect in these kinds of Foster Care Homes, but I gave it a try. A married lady Elsa Atis ran the home. I was surprised when I met the her that she was the only employee of the care home and found out she had worked as a nurse assistant for 15 years in various nursing homes. She had decided to go out on her own and run her own 'Elsa Atis Foster Care Home facility.' Her husband worked at Schofield Barracks, and she had three children. The oldest girl was a working RN, a son who was in nursing school in Las Vegas, and a daughter who was in 7th Grade. Elsa was making enough money to put her kids through college.

I was also pleasantly surprised at the quality of the home. The remodeling was well done. The house was clean, clutter-free, and extremely organized. The best surprise was the private room available which was immaculate and neatly furnished with a hospital bed, lounge chair, chest of drawers, TV, air conditioning, and a large closet. There was a bathroom next door, along with a shower. The cost was half of the nursing home, and the almost one-on-one attention convinced me that this was the place for Luci. Luci got her new home on April 22, 2019, and has been there ever since.

Chapter 49

Living Anew

I was finally given a break (Thank God!) and was starting to feel healthy again. I resumed exercising, walking not running, and working out in the condo gym. I Nam and I were living together. I had moral and mixed emotions about that living situation. I talked to a priest about the situation and living condition and when I told him that it had been a sexual situation before, it was now "Platonic" since I was too old. He said as long as I didn't abandon Luci and keep visiting her, which I always had planned to do, I couldn't abandon her! He approved my relationship with I Nam and our living situation.

My only defense for the situation I found myself is that for years since it became obvious that Luci was destined for some type of care home, I feared that I would be living alone, and I would die alone. It seems like I should be comfortable being alone since I was an only child, whose parents both worked. Despite that, I am deathly afraid of being alone and dying alone, period. I have the strong feeling that God sent I Nam to me and I thank Him daily. She has turned out to be a loving partner and friend. We go to church together and pray together. We have saved each other, and we recognize our blessings and we are very happy together. Although born and raised as a Buddhist, she is now a devout Catholic and a very balanced and happy person. So am I.

It happened!

Someone asked me recently what I said to I Nam to convince her to enter the Catholic Church. My answer simply is, "I didn't say anything to her. I think it was mostly the way I live my life and the example I gave to her especially toward Luci.." She also had those previous exposures to the Catholic faith when she went to mass with her girlfriend. She daily says she loves me and it blossomed because of how I take care of Luci, visit her and continue to love her.

I am now living out the last years of my life with one of the nicest and most loving and talented persons I have ever met.

"I will send people to you."

Chapter 50

Endings and Beginnings

I have never felt that saving or accumulating money was important so that my children would have an inheritance. It was just not the right thing to do in my mind. Our children all have college educations and are doing well in the world. Along the way, I have helped Ron Jr., Michael, and Sharon with money to help them in their immediate needs.

Debby never asked me for financial help.

With all of this in mind, I have given title to one of my two Condo properties to I Nam as well as access to my accounts at the NFCU. On the other side, she is always giving me money. She has worked hard all her life with little to show for it, but now with my property and monetary gifts, she will not have to worry financially about her old age and eventual retirement after I am gone.

I wish to have my ashes to be buried at the cemetery in Blooming Prairie, Minnesota next to my parents. I also wish for Luci's ashes to be buried beside me in the same plot in Blooming Prairie, Minnesota. I Nam wants to be buried in Korea.

So Thankful for Your Love and Mercy, my Lord and my God.

Please forgive me for all the mistakes I have made.

And remember how I served You.

+

When you hear His voice, harden not your heart.

THE END

Made in the USA
Las Vegas, NV
28 May 2024

90467635R00066